STUDY GUIDE

MANAGERIAL ACCOUNTING:
AN INTRODUCTION TO CONCEPTS, METHODS, AND USES
Third Edition

STUDY GUIDE

Anne J. Rich, Ph.D., CPA, CMA
University of Bridgeport

MANAGERIAL ACCOUNTING:
AN INTRODUCTION TO CONCEPTS, METHODS, AND USES
Third Edition

Sidney Davidson, Ph.D., CPA
University of Chicago

Michael W. Maher, Ph.D., CPA
University of California - Davis

Clyde P. Stickney, D.B.A., CPA
Dartmouth College

Roman L. Weil, Ph.D., CPA, CMA
University of Chicago

THE DRYDEN PRESS
Chicago   New York   San Francisco
Philadelphia   Montreal   Toronto
London   Sydney   Tokyo

ISBN 0-03-011959-6
Printed in the United States of America
890-018-987654321

Copyright © 1988, 1985 by The Dryden Press, a division of
Holt, Rinehart and Winston, Inc.

All rights reserved. No part of this publication may
be reproduced or transmitted in any form or by any means,
electronic or mechanical, including photocopy, recording,
or any information storage and retrieval system, without
permission in writing from the publisher.

Although for mechanical reasons all pages of this publication
are perforated, only those pages imprinted with The Dryden Press
copyright notice are intended for removal.

Requests for permission to make copies of any part of
the work should be mailed to: Permissions, Holt, Rinehart
and Winston, Inc., 111 Fifth Avenue, New York, New York 10003.

Address orders:
111 Fifth Avenue
New York, NY 10003

Address editorial correspondence:
One Salt Creek Lane
Hinsdale, IL 60521

The Dryden Press
Holt, Rinehart and Winston
Saunders College Publishing

FORWARD TO THE STUDENT

This study guide is designed to supplement <u>Managerial Accounting: An Introduction to Concepts, Methods, and Uses</u>, Third Edition, by Sidney Davidson, Michael W. Maher, Clyde P. Stickney, and Roman L. Weil. A number of self-test and practice exercises are presented for each chapter, making it possible to use this study guide in conjunction with the text as a self-teaching package.

Organization of the Book

This study guide contains nineteen chapters. The first eighteen chapters correspond to the eighteen chapters in the text. Chapter 19 corresponds to the appendix. The sixteenth chapter presents a comprehensive review, including an outline of the entire text. This chapter is a valuable framework for study at the beginning or at the conclusion of the course.

Organization of the Chapters

Each chapter in this study guide is generally structured according to the following pattern of organization:

1. The chapter contents are summarized briefly.

2. Next, the major topics are highlighted in narrative form. You may find it useful to read this section before reading the text in order to get a feeling for the chapter material. This section also serves as a review when you have completed reading the chapter in the text. In this manner, you will have reinforced your understanding of the concepts and techniques introduced to you, chapter by chapter.

3. The third section consists of self-test and practice exercises. Accounting concepts are best understood when they are applied to specific situations. This section typically includes matching exercises to help you learn new terms and short, simple problems that will help you complete the exercises and problems in the text.

4. The fourth section contains the solutions to the study guide exercises. These give immediate feedback and direct your attention to areas that need additional attention.

5. The fifth section presents a study plan. The plan points to particular exhibits in the text that should be reviewed and identifies particular self-study problems that could be reworked with new information. Specific exercises found in the text that follow logically from the study guide problems are also identified.

6. Finally, the chapter is reviewed briefly in outline form. At this point, you should be familiar with all the terms and concepts.

Acknowledgments

I would like to thank Professor Michael W. Maher for his input in the preparation of this Study Guide. Mr. Woo-Yong Yum and Mr. Sanjay Sharma reviewed the material and made many helpful comments. I also thank Mr. Michael Reynolds for his support and overall supervision of this project.

                                                           A.J.R.

CONTENTS

Chapter 1 The Management Process and Accounting Information....1

Chapter 2 Cost Concepts and Behavior..........................14

Chapter 3 Product Costing Methods.............................24

Chapter 4 Accounting for Resource Flows: Cost Accumulation....38

Chapter 5 Cost Allocation.....................................50

Chapter 6 Estimating Cost Behavior............................61

Chapter 7 Cost-Volume-Profit Analysis.........................72

Chapter 8 Short-Run Decisions and Differential Analysis.......87

Chapter 9 Long-Run Decisions and Capital Budgeting...........101

Chapter 10 Capital Budgeting: A Closer Look...................113

Chapter 11 Planning, Control, and Incentives 128

Chapter 12 Operating Budgets..................................137

Chapter 13 Measuring and Interpreting Variances...............151

Chapter 14 Measuring and Interpreting Variances: Additional
           Topics...159

Chapter 15 Divisional Performance Measurement and Control.....170

Chapter 16 Synthesis: Managerial Accounting and External
           Reporting..184

Chapter 17 Overview of Financial Statements...................197

Chapter 18 Analysis of Financial Statements...................208

Chapter 19 Compound Interest Examples and Applications......218

CHAPTER 1

THE MANAGEMENT PROCESS AND ACCOUNTING INFORMATION

The first chapter presents an overview of the management accounting process and the environment in which management and financial accounting operate. The general approach to rational decision making is discussed. The planning and control process which is the central theme in the development and use of management accounting systems is also presented. The chapter then identifies the similarities and differences between financial and managerial accounting. Finally, the chapter introduces one of the major themes of accounting: the cost-benefit approach of obtaining information for management decisions.

CHAPTER HIGHLIGHTS

A. Accounting is part of an organization's information system, which includes both financial and nonfinancial data. Common uses of accounting data are (1) **financial accounting** and (2) **managerial accounting**.

B. Financial accounting refers to the generation of general-purpose reports for use by persons outside the organization. These persons are called external users and include (1) **stockholders** or owners of the organization (2) **creditors** or those who lend money to the organization (3) **labor unions** (4) government **regulators**.

C. Management accounting provides information to individuals inside the organization. Managers of all kinds of organizations, (manufacturing, retail, service and not-for-profit), need information to make decisions. Often general-purpose financial statements do not provide sufficient detail or the right format for management decisions. Managerial accounting focuses on information which will aid managers in making decisions, and in planning and controlling business operations.

D. Since financial accounting provides outsiders with information about the firm's financial performance consistent with generally accepted accounting principles (GAAP), and managerial accounting aids managers in making decisions and in planning, controlling, and evaluating internal performance, accounting is said to have three general uses, namely (1) **financial reporting and external performance evaluation**, (2) **managerial decision making**, (3) **managerial planning, control, and internal performance evaluation**.

E. When managers make decisions, five steps should be followed: (1) **identify the problem**, (2) **specify a goal or objective**, (3) **list possible alternatives**,

(4) obtain information concerning the probable outcomes of each alternative, and (5) make a decision.

The concept of **return on investment** is very important to managers, creditors, and investors. Return on investment (ROI) is the return on an investment (as opposed to the return of the original principal amount). Accounting ROI is calculated by dividing accounting income by investment. (There are numerous ways to define and to measure the investment.) Economic ROI substitutes net cash flows (cash revenues less cash expenses) for accounting income.

The long-range goal of managers is to maximize the return on the stockholders' investment over a long period of time. This is accomplished by generating cash flows from the business activity. In the short-run, managers often make decisions by selecting the alternative that generates the highest cash flow for each dollar invested. Managerial accounting plays a critical role in obtaining information on the probable cash flows associated with each alternative identified by managers.

F. The planning and control process includes three steps: (1) **specifying a criterion as to what actual performance should be**, (2) **measuring the results of actual performance**, and (3) **evaluating performance by comparing actual performance with the criterion.**

A budget is an example of a device used to plan the operations of a firm. As actual expenses are made, they can be compared against the budget to help managers control the cash flow of the firm. Internal performance evaluation includes regular comparisons of budgets to actual performance.

G. Financial accounting provides information to investors and creditors in evaluating the firm's performance. Investors and creditors will compare firms based on publicly available financial reports that must conform to generally accepted accounting principles. Managers must be aware of how external users will interpret financial information presented to them. Often managers will work hard to make the financial reports look good without economic substance supporting their decisions. For continued support from the investors and creditors, managers must make decisions that are economically sound. In turn, the financial reports should reflect as realistically as possible the economic consequences of the decisions managers made. However, since financial accounting reports must follow accrual concepts while managers focus on cash flows, sometimes a manager may make a good decision that is reported as a bad decision, at least in the short-run.

H. While managerial and financial accounting reports have the goal of providing useful information, there are some fundamental differences between managerial and financial accounting. Financial accounting is directed to external users (stockholders, creditors, and financial analysts); must comply with generally accepted accounting principles (GAAP); looks backwards to transactions that have actually taken place (historical data); is controlled by outside regulatory agencies; and data is presented in summary form. Managerial accounting is directed towards internal users (mainly managers); can be creative and does not need to conform to generally accepted accounting principles; focuses not only on historic information but also on estimates of what will happen in the future; and the types and timing of reports are determined by managers themselves. For example, managers need more detailed data about product costs, revenues, and profits than stockhoders.

I. Managerial accounting should be user-driven. Managers should first identify the problems, goals, and alternatives and then obtain the information appropriate for decision making.

J. Accounting functions within the organization include the positions of controller, internal auditor, and treasurer. The **controller** is the chief accounting official and oversees the preparation of external and internal financial reports. The **internal auditor** evaluates accounting controls and reports on the effectiveness of accounting procedures (operational audits). The **treasurer** manages cash and near cash assets as well as obtains financing for the company.

K. There are numerous regulatory bodies affecting accounting reports to external users. The Securities and Exchange Commission (SEC), a governmental agency, requires special reports for many publicly held companies in order to protect investors. The **Financial Accounting Standards Board** (FASB) and the **American Institute of Certified Public Accountants** (AICPA) direct the standards for general purpose financial reports to outsiders. These are private organizations that get support from the accounting profession. The Internal Revenue Service, (IRS) the government's tax agency, sometimes impacts financial reporting by requiring accounting records to conform to tax rules. The Cost Accounting Standards Board (CASB), a governmental agency, has set standards for companies that have contracts to make products for the federal government.

L. There are two major certification programs for American accountants. The **Certified Public Accountant** (CPA) is necessary to certify that financial statements conform to generally accepted accounting principles. CPAs also provide tax and consulting advice. The organization that sponsors the national examination is the American Institute of Certified Public Accountants; however, each state has its own rules to qualify for a license to practice public accountancy. The **Certified Management Accountant** (CMA) is a professional designation for managerial accountants. The organization that sponsors the CMA is the National Association of Accountants (NAA).

In Canada, two organizations provide similar designations. The Canadian Institute of Chartered Accountants (CICA) provides the **Chartered Accountant** (CA) and the Certified General Accountants Association of Canada (CGAA) gives the **Certified General Accountant** (CGA) designation. The Society of Management Accountants gives a Certified Management Accountant (CMA) designation similar to the CMA in the U.S.

M. When making decisions, accounting information is essential in quantifying the costs and benefits associated with each alternative. While there may be some difficulty in measuring all the costs and benefits, at a minimum, the manager must identify cash outflows and inflows. If the cash inflow is greater than the cash outflow, we often conclude that the benefits have exceeded the costs.

N. Since information costs money to obtain and analyze, managers must compare the value of the new information received with the cost of generating that new information. Like all managerial projects, if the new information can improve the net cash flow of the firm, then it should be acquired.

SELF-TEST AND PRACTICE EXERCISES

The answers are found after the last exercise in each chapter.

A. MATCHING

Match each of the following terms with its meaning.

Term	Meaning
___ 1. Financial accounting	a. A private organization supported by professional accountants that establishes standards for financial reporting.
___ 2. Certified Public Accountant	b. The person who exercises control over both external and internal accounting reports for an organization.
___ 3. Controller	c. A governmental agency that protects investors by requiring special accounting reports.
___ 4. Managerial accounting	d. The comparison of cash inflows and cash outflows to determine which alternative to select.
___ 5. SEC	e. A licensed person who can certify that financial statements conform to accounting standards.
___ 6. Internal audit department	f. Accounting standards that have gained acceptance by the accounting profession.
___ 7. GAAP	g. The designation of the National Association of Accountants to recognize excellence in management accounting.
___ 8. Certified Management Accountant	h. The department in organizations that audits internal controls and evaluates the effectiveness of procedures.
___ 9. FASB	i. The discipline that prepares reports to managers.
___ 10. Cost/benefit criterion	j. The discipline that prepares reports for stockholders and creditors.

B. DECISION MAKING

B. J. Smith, a college student, needs a summer job. He wants to work in the data processing industry. He is trying to decide whether to take a course that will teach him computer skills. He has identified the following two alternatives: (1) take a course in the business school at a cost of $500 for tuition and books or (2) take a course in the adult education program at a cost of $260 plus $25 for books. The course in the business school will allow him to get a part-time summer job as a programmer earning $2,000 for the summer. The adult education course will only prepare him for a data entry job for the summer and his pay will be $1,000.

REQUIRED:

1. What is Smith's objective? _____

2. What are his alternatives?

   (a) _____

   (b) _____

   (c) _____

3. What are the quantifiable and nonquantifiable costs associated with each alternative?

   (a) quantifiable costs _____

   (b) nonquantifiable costs _____

4. What are the quantifiable benefits associated with each alternative? What are the nonquantifiable benefits?

   (a) quantifiable benefits _____

   (b) nonquantifiable benefits _____

5. What decision should Smith make? _____

6. Would more information help him make a better decision?

   _____

   _____

   _____

C. BUSINESS DECISION MAKING

Upon graduating from college, B. J. Smith and N. E. Jones decided they would open their own computer consulting business. They needed external financing in order to buy equipment.

REQUIRED:

1. What information would a banker need in order to evaluate whether the two entrepreneurs should get a bank loan?

   _____

   _____

   _____

2. Suppose a friend said she had money in the bank but was willing to invest in the business if it were a sound investment. What information would the friend need in order to decide to take her money out of the bank and invest it the consulting business?

   _____

   _____

   _____

3. Explain the concept of return on investment.

   _____

   _____

   _____

   _____

D. HISTORIC FINANCIAL STATEMENTS AND MANAGERIAL ACCOUNTING

   Donna White owns a share of stock in two companies. Every year Donna White receives an annual report from these companies. She notices that the return on investment of one was 16% while the other was only 8%. She knows the bank is offering a rate of interest of 10%. She wonders whether she should sell only the stock that earned an 8% return, or sell both shares and put her money in the bank.

   REQUIRED:

   1. What factors should she consider before making her decision?

   _____

   _____

   2. What are the limitations of financial statements prepared using generally accepted accounting principles?

   _____

   _____

SOLUTIONS

A. MATCHING:

   1. j   4. i   7. f   10. d
   2. e   5. c   8. g
   3. b   6. h   9. a

B. DECISION MAKING:

   1. Smith's objective is to get a summer job in the data processing industry.

   2. His alternatives are (a) take a course in order to work as a programmer, (b) take a course in order to work as a data entry clerk and (c) try to find a job without taking a course.

   3. (a) Quantifiable costs include tuition and books.
      (b) Nonquantifiable costs include his time in the course and in doing homework.

   4. (a) Quantifiable benefits include his pay for the summer.
      (b) Nonquantifiable benefits include his job satisfaction and the potential for future summer and post-graduation employment.

5. If Smith's decision is based only on maximizing his pay for the summer, he would analyze his alternatives as follows:

   Alternative A (work as a programmer) benefits amount to $2,000 and costs $500. Therefore benefits exceed the cost by $1,500 ($2,000 less $500).

   Alternative B (work as a data entry clerk) benefits amount to $1,000 and costs $285 ($260 plus $25). Therefore benefits exceed the cost by $715 ($1,000 less $285).

   Alternative C needs more information, but he can assume that without training he will not get a job in this field.

   Alternative A (work as a programmer) has the highest benefit/cost ratio.

6. Yes. If Smith preferred his free time and only needed $715 pay for the summer, he might have chosen alternative B. In addition, Smith has not considered the future potential earnings power of each career nor the opportunity for summer or permanent employment in the future.

C. BUSINESS DECISION MAKING:

1. A banker would need a projected statement of financial position, projected income statements and projected cash flow statements in order to determine whether or not the business venture has the capacity to pay back the loan and the interest on the borrowed money. In addition, the banker would need nonfinancial information such as location, competition, and the experience of the managers. Bankers also request personal financial statements of the prospective owners.

2. The friend would require the same information, however, if she were an equity investor, she would have to assess the amount and timing of dividends to be paid to her.

3. Return on investment is the income that is paid to investors as a percentage of the amount they invested.

D. HISTORIC FINANCIAL STATEMENTS AND MANAGERIAL ACCOUNTING:

1. Her preference for liquidity, her need for a predictable return on her investment, and the future earning power of each of the companies compared to what is likely to happen to interest rates are the factors she should consider before making any investment decision.

2. Financial statements are historic in nature and do not provide information on future events that will affect the entity.

STUDY PLAN

1. Review the problem for self-study in the text. You should understand the term ROI. Why is an alternative to the use of ROI the comparison of cash inflows and outflows?

2. Try to do problem 16 in the text. This problem highlights the differences between managerial decision making and the financial reporting of the actions managers take. Compare your analysis with the following detailed solution:

Year 1: <u>Operating profit</u>	Keep old car	Buy new car
Revenues: (1)		
Less Expenses:		
Operating costs (2)	-1,200	
Depreciation (3)	0	-1,300
Gain on disposal (4)		+ 300
Effect on net income	-1,200	-1,000

Year 1: <u>Cash flows</u>		
Revenues: (1)		
Less Expenses:		
Operating costs (2)	-1,200	
Depreciation (5)	0	0
Purchase of new taxi		-7,000
Proceeds from sale of old taxi		+ 300
Effect on cash flow	-1,200	-6,700

(1) We don't know the absolute amount of revenue, we only know that there would be no difference in revenues. Either substitute an arbitrary, but equal, amount for revenue in both cases or ignore it because it won't affect the analysis.

(2) The same reasoning for operating expenses as for revenues. Since we only know that the difference will be $1,200, either substitute an arbitrary, but different, by $1,200, amount for expenses, or work with the $1,200 difference.

(3) We are assuming straight-line depreciation for an asset with a cost of $7,000, a salvage value of $500, and a useful life of 5 years [$7,000-500)/5].

(4) Since the book value of the old taxi is zero, the gain on the disposal would be equal to the proceeds of $300.

(5) Depreciation has no effect on cash flows.

3. Review the following outline. By now all the material should be familiar to you.

REVIEW OUTLINE

I. Accounting is part of an organization's information system. (See Exhibit 1.1)

II. Accounting is often divided into financial and managerial accounting.

   A. Financial accounting refers to the generation of general-purpose reports for use by persons outside the organization.

   B. Managerial accounting includes the providing of information to managers inside the organization. Managers of all kinds of organizations, (manufacturing, retail, service and not-for-profit), need information to make decisions. In addition to analyzing historic information, managers must make estimates about future events. (See Exhibit 1.2)

III. There are three uses of accounting information.

   A. Financial reporting and external performance evaluation

      1. Financial reports must conform to generally accepted accounting principles (GAAP).

      2. Financial reports are historic in nature and provide little information on the future course of the entity.

   B. Managerial decision making

      1. The decision-making process is described in five steps:

         a. Identify the problem requiring action.
         b. Specify the goal or objective to be achieved.
         c. List the possible alternative courses of action.
         d. Gather information about the consequences of each alternative.
         e. Make a decision.

      2. Managerial accounting plays a critical role in quantifying the cash inflows and outflows associated with alternative opportunities.

   C. Managerial planning, control, and internal performance evaluation

      The planning and control process includes three steps:

         a. Specifying a criterion as to what the actual performance should be (the plan).

                b. Measuring the results of actual performance.
                c. Evaluating performance by comparing actual performance
                   with the criterion.

IV. Comparison of managerial and financial accounting.

    A. Managerial and financial accounting often report consistent, complimentary results of operations and financial position of an organization.

    B. While managerial and financial accounting reports have the goal of providing useful information, there are some fundamental differences between managerial and financial accounting.

        1. Financial accounting is directed to external users (stockholders, creditors and financial analysts).

            a. It must comply with generally accepted accounting principles (GAAP).
            b. It looks backward to transactions that have actually taken place (historical data).
            c. It is controlled by outside regulatory agencies.
            d. Information is usually presented in summary form.

        2. Managerial accounting is directed to internal users (mainly managers).

            a. It can be creative.
            b. It does not need to conform to generally accepted accounting principles.
            c. It focuses not only on historic information but also on estimates of what will happen in the future.
            d. The types and timing of reports are determined by managers themselves.
            e. Reports are usually more detailed.

V. The environment of managerial and financial accounting.

    A. Accounting functions within the organization include the controller, internal auditor, and treasurer.

    B. There are numerous regulatory bodies affecting accounting reports to external users.

        1. The Securities and Exchange Commission (SEC).
        2. The Financial Accounting Standards Board (FASB) and the American Institute of Certified Public Accountants (AICPA).
        3. The Internal Revenue Service (IRS).
        4. The Cost Accounting Standards Board (CASB). (It no longer exists but its standards must be followed).

C. There are two key concepts in managerial accounting.

   1. Cost/Benefit criterion -- decisions are made when the benefits exceed the cost.

   2. Value of information -- decisions are made to obtain more information when it is determined that the company will benefit by an amount more than the information costs.

D. Return on investment (ROI).

   1. Accounting ROI is calculated by dividing accounting income by investment.

   2. Economic ROI utilizes net cash flows in place of accounting income.

   3. There are alternative definitions and measurements of investment.

E. There are two certification programs for American accountants.

   1. The Certified Public Accountant (CPA).

   2. The Certified Management Accountant (CMA).

F. In Canada, examinations and certifications are given by the Canadian Institute of Chartered Accountants and the Certified General Accountants Association as well as the Society of Management Accountants.

CHAPTER 2

COST CONCEPTS AND BEHAVIOR

In this chapter, alternative ways the term cost is used in practice is introduced. Basic cost behavior patterns are presented. In addition, variable costing and full absorption costing are explained and components of unit costs are identified.

CHAPTER HIGHLIGHTS

A. Managers need information concerning the costs of operating an organization. Costs are sacrifices of resources.

B. To be meaningful, the term cost must be applied in a particular context. The **time dimension** is important. That is, is the cost an average historic cost, a current cost to replace an item of inventory or a future inflation-adjusted cost?

C. In economics and in accounting, the **opportunity cost** concept assists us in making rational decisions. The opportunity cost is defined as the cost of using an asset for an alternative use other than the best one for it. It is the cost a company must bear if it chooses not to make the best use of its resources. Managers sometimes choose to bear this cost in current periods in order to achieve their long-run strategic goals.

D. **Costs**, or sacrifices, are important managerial terms. In managerial accounting, we are concerned with costs, and not with expenses. In financial accounting, expenses (or expired assets) are measured in order to prepare financial statements consistent with **generally accepted accounting principles** (GAAP).

E. A useful classification of costs includes direct and indirect costs. **Direct costs** are related to a cost object and need no special allocation. **Indirect costs**, on the other hand, must be allocated by a formula in order to be associated with a cost object. It is possible for an item to be considered direct to one cost object and indirect to another. For example, rent is direct to a sales office but is indirect to the products sold from that office. Thus, it is important to first identify the cost object, and then, to classify the cost.

F. **Common costs** are indirect costs shared by two or more cost objects. Usually a cost is indirect because it is considered a common cost that must be allocated to two or more cost objects. For example, the salary of a supervisor who is responsible for two departments, is first allocated to each department because it is a common cost, and then each product produced within each department is made to absorb some of the indirect salary allocated to the department.

G. There are three basic types of profit-oriented organizations: service, retail, and manufacturing. Of the three, manufacturing is most complex because it involves determining the cost of the items produced.

H. The cost of a manufactured unit includes its **direct materials**, **direct labor**, and **manufacturing overhead**. The term **prime costs** refers to the essential inputs, direct materials, and direct labor. The term **conversion costs** refers to the elements necessary to convert the materials into its final form, namely, direct labor and manufacturing overhead.

I. **Nonmanufacturing costs** include marketing costs and general administrative costs. The income statement will show these costs separate from the product costs.

J. Following GAAP, costs attach to assets first. Then, consistent with the matching principle, expired assets are expensed during the period. Manufacturing costs attach to the asset called inventory and are referred to as **product costs**. When the inventory is sold, the expense for the period is referred to as the **cost of goods sold**. Costs assigned to other assets that expire are called **period costs**.

K. One of the most useful classifications for managerial decision making is the distinction between fixed and variable costs. **Variable costs** increase in total as some activity increases. A **fixed cost** remains constant over a wide range of activity. While both costs are defined in relation to their behavior over some volume, it is important to understand the impact on per unit costs: variable costs are constant per unit; fixed costs decrease per unit as activity increases. The cost behavior is valid over a relevant range of activity.

L. Fixed costs are considered fixed only over the short-run, about a year.

M. The operating profit of a company is the result of sales revenue less the company's fixed and variable expenses. Sales revenue can be expressed as the selling price per unit multiplied by the number of units (P)(x). Total variable costs can be expressed as the variable costs per unit multiplied by the number of units (V)(x). Fixed costs can be expressed as a lump sum for the period (F). Thus, operating profits (π) can be computed by using the following formula:

$$\pi = Px - Vx - F$$

N. The point at which the total cost (total variable plus fixed) equals the total revenue is known as the breakeven point. The breakeven point, in units, can be found by setting profits equal to zero in the above equation. When solving for x, the breakeven formula can be written as:

$$x = F/(P-V)$$

O. The breakeven formula can be rewritten in terms of the contribution margin. The contribution margin per unit (CM) is what is left over from every unit sale after the variable costs are covered. Thus, the contribution margin is sales price per unit (P) less variable costs per unit (V). The breakeven formula can be rewritten as:

$$x = F/CM$$

P. In decision making, it is easier to focus on **differential costs**, or **incremental costs**, or those costs that would be affected if a contemplated action is taken. This will reduce the amount of data to be analyzed. Normally, variable costs will change if volume changes. However, variable costs will not change if volume doesn't change. Fixed costs usually do not change in the short-run. However, if they do differ between the alternatives, they would be considered differential costs.

Q. The distinction between period and product costs is important in calculating operating profits. Product costs are costs that attach to inventory. Period costs are costs that are expensed in the current accounting period. Product costs become expenses through the cost of goods sold formula.

R. The only acceptable financial reporting standard is that inventories be assigned their full absorption cost and that the difference between the cost of goods sold and sales revenue be referred to as gross profit. In managerial accounting, variable costing may be used. In variable costing, the difference between the sales revenue and the variable costs is called the contribution margin.

S. There are numerous cost definitions and concepts. Neither the full absorption nor variable cost concept includes marketing and administrative expenses in inventory valuations. However, the concept of the full cost of a product should include the product's marketing and administrative costs.

T. Sunk costs are costs already incurred. Regardless of any future action, these costs cannot be changed. Managers should ignore sunk costs and make decisions based solely on future costs that will change between the alternatives (the differential costs).

U. The concept of controllability is important for assigning costs to the people responsible for them.

SELF-TEST AND PRACTICE EXERCISES

A. MATCHING

Match each of the following terms with its meaning.

Term	Meaning
___1. Differential cost	a. The sum of direct labor and manufacturing overhead.
___2. Opportunity cost	b. Cost that changes as activity changes.
___3. Direct cost	c. Incremental costs and decremental costs.
___4. Indirect cost	d. Cost that needs no allocation.
___5. Prime costs	e. Includes direct materials, direct labor, and manufacturing overhead.
___6. Conversion costs	f. An expenditure that does not vary with volume.
___7. Manufacturing costs	g. Cost that needs to be allocated to a cost object.
___8. Fixed cost	h. Sum of direct materials and direct labor.
___9. Period cost	i. The value of the best alternative to the one being considered.
__10. Variable cost	j. Expired assets.

B. IDENTIFICATION OF COST TERMS

    Robert Baker, a marketing major, had to decide which course to enroll in during the summer semester. He noted that a computer course he wanted to take was offered at a cost of $600 plus fees for computer time charged at the rate of $25 per hour. His other choice was a management course. The tuition for the management course was $850 because of a field trip requirement. In addition to selecting a course, Robert needed a place to stay during the summer. While he already paid $1,000 for a dormitory room, Robert decided he no longer could live with his roommate. There were two rooms available: a private residence that would cost him $1,400 and a semi-private room that would cost $1,100. Robert could sublet his dormitory but feels he should keep it empty in case he changes his mind and wants to return to campus.

REQUIRED: Identify the following:

1) a sunk cost _____

    _____

2) an opportunity cost _____

    _____

3) a fixed cost _____

    _____

4) a variable cost _____

    _____

5) a differential cost _____

    _____

C. FULL ABSORPTION AND VARIABLE COSTING

The Ambose Company makes a single product. Assume the following facts:

Units produced during the year	2,000 units
Variable manufacturing cost per unit:	
Direct materials	$2.00 per unit
Direct labor	$1.50 per unit
Variable manufacturing overhead	$1.00 per unit
Fixed manufacturing costs:	$5,000 per year
Marketing and Administrative	
Fixed costs	$3,000 per year
Variable costs	$3.00 per unit

REQUIRED:

1. What is the full absorption cost for inventory following generally accepted accounting principles for inventory costing?

   _____

2. What is the fully allocated cost for managerial decision-making purposes?

   _____

3. What is the total direct manufacturing cost per unit?_____

4. What is the total indirect manufacturing cost per unit?_____

5. What is the total variable cost per unit?_____

6. What is the total fixed cost per unit?_____

7. What variable costs attach to the inventory under the concept of variable costing?

   _____

D. BREAKEVEN ANALYSIS

In Exercise C, if the sales price is $10 per unit, determine (1) the contribution margin and (2) the breakeven point in units.

SOLUTIONS

A. MATCHING:

1. c   2. i   3. d   4. g   5. h

6. a   7. e   8. f   9. j   10. b

B. IDENTIFICATION OF COST TERMS:

(1) The rent for the dormitory he no longer wishes to occupy is a sunk cost.

(2) The foregone rent from subletting his dormitory is an example of an opportunity cost.

(3) His monthly rent is a fixed cost.

(4) The hourly charge for computer time is a variable cost.

(5) The difference in tuition between the courses, as well as the difference in rent for the new housing, are differential costs.

C. FULL ABSORPTION AND VARIABLE COSTING:

(1) The full absorption cost is determined by adding the variable manufacturing cost per unit and the fixed manufacturing cost per unit. The variable manufacturing costs are direct labor, direct materials, and variable overhead ($2.00 + $1.50 + $1.00 = $4.50 per unit). The fixed manufacturing cost per unit is determined by dividing total manufacturing cost by the number of units produced ($5,000/2,000 units = $2.50 per unit). Thus, the full absorption cost is $7.00 ($4.50 + $2.50).

(2) For managerial decision-making purposes, marketing costs are considered part of the overall cost to produce and sell the product. Therefore, variable and fixed marketing costs per unit must be added to the manufacturing cost. In this example, variable marketing costs are $3.00 per unit and fixed costs are $1.50 ($3,000/2,000 units). The full cost of producing and selling this product is $7.00 (manufacturing cost per unit) + $4.50 (marketing cost per unit), or $11.50.

(3) Direct materials ($2.00) + direct labor ($1.50) = $3.50 per unit @ 2,000 units, or $7,000 in total.

(4) Indirect manufacturing costs include variable manufacturing overhead, $1.00 per unit, and fixed manufacturing overhead, $2.50 per unit ($5,000/2,000 units) for a total of $3.50 per unit.

(5)
Variable manufacturing cost per unit	$4.50
Variable marketing cost per unit	3.00
Total variable cost per unit	$7.50

(6) Fixed manufacturing cost $5,000
    Fixed marketing cost   3,000
    Total fixed cost $8,000
    No. of units   2,000
    Fixed cost/no. of units $4.00 per unit

(7) Under variable inventory costing, only the direct materials ($2.00), direct labor ($1.50), and variable overhead ($1.00), attach to the product cost, for a total cost per unit of $4.50.

D. BREAKEVEN:

(1) $2.50. The contribution margin is the sales price ($10.00) less the variable costs. The variable costs are direct materials ($2.00), direct labor ($1.50), variable manufacturing overhead ($1.00), and variable marketing and administrative costs ($3.00). Thus, $10 less $7.50 is $2.50.

(2) 3,200 units. The breakeven point is the point where fixed costs equal the contribution margin multiplied by the number of units produced and sold. Thus, in the equation x = F/CM, where F = $8,000 (the sum of $5,000 + $3,000) and the contribution margin per unit is $2.50, then the number of units needed to breakeven is 3,200.

STUDY PLAN

1. Do both self-study problems.

2. Try to solve Exercise 28. Did you reach the correct answer? If not, review the following detailed solution:

   A. This problem suggests the use of differential analysis: that is, focus on the elements that will change between the alternatives. There is no need to do the entire income statement again. A special order for 400 units would not reduce regular sales, therefore, the current level of profit is irrelevant and can be ignored. Similarly, the special order would not increase the fixed costs because the company has the capacity to produce 2,500 units, and is currently producing only 2,000. Thus, the 400 units can be produced using the existing capacity and fixed costs will remain unchanged. The only elements that will change are the sales revenue and the variable costs (manufacturing and sales commissions). The calculations are as follows:

        Incremental sales revenue (400 units @ $32) $12,800
        Incremental costs (all variable)
           Manufacturing (400 units @ $24) $9,600
           Sales commissions (400 @ $1.25)*   500   10,100
        Addition to company profit $ 2,700

* Sales commissions are one-half of the normal $2.50 per unit.

B. What would happen if a special, one-time setup cost of $500 was required for the special order? Answer: This would be an incremental fixed cost that would reduce the addition to company profit by $500.

  C. What would happen if the special order was for 600 units? Answer: We do not know except that the company is beyond its capacity. We would have to estimate the costs of new facilities or subcontract the work.

3. Review the following outline. Be sure you understand the meaning of all the terms introduced in the chapter. The glossary is a useful reference.

REVIEW OUTLINE

I. Costs and expenses.

  A. Costs are sacrifices of resources.

  B. Opportunity cost concept is the cost of using an asset for a purpose other than the best alternative use of it.

  C. Expenses are expired assets.

II. Direct and indirect costs.

  A. Costs related directly to a cost object are called direct costs.

  B. Costs that must be allocated to a cost object are called indirect costs.

  C. When indirect costs are common to, or shared by, two or more cost objects, they are called common costs.

III. Manufacturing costs.

  A. Product costs include direct materials, direct labor, and manufacturing overhead.

  B. Prime costs include only direct materials and direct labor.

  C. Conversion costs include direct labor and manufacturing overhead.

IV. Nonmanufacturing costs.

  A. Nonmanufacturing costs include marketing and administrative costs.

  B. Nonmanufacturing costs never attach to the product cost.

V. Cost behavior. (You should refer to Exhibit 2.2 in the text).

   A. Variable costs.

      1. Variable costs change as the volume of activity changes and are zero when production is zero.

      2. Variable costs per unit are constant over a wide range of activity.

   B. Fixed costs.

      1. Fixed costs remain constant during an accounting period within a reasonable range of activity (sometimes called the relevant range).

      2. Fixed cost per unit decreases as activity (or volume) increases.

VI. Breakeven analysis using the contribution margin concept.

   A. The point at which a company does not make a profit nor incurs a loss is called the breakeven point.

   B. The contribution margin is the sales price per unit less the variable costs per unit.

   C. Breakeven can be computed by dividing fixed costs by the contribution margin per unit.

VII. Differential costs.

   A. Analysis of differences between alternatives is called differential analysis.

   B. Incremental as well as decremental costs should be considered.

   C. Changes in fixed costs as well as variable costs should be considered.

   D. Focuses on only those elements that change makes the analysis easier.

   E. Sunk costs result from past expenditures and should not be considered in making current decisions.

VIII. Income reporting.

   A. GAAP requires the income statement be presented by reporting sales revenue, cost of goods sold (using absorption costing), gross margin, marketing and administrative expenses, and net operating income.

   B. For managerial decision making, a contribution format is preferred showing sales revenue, variable cost of goods sold, other variable expenses, contribution margin, fixed manufacturing and marketing costs, and operating profit.

CHAPTER 3

PRODUCT COSTING METHODS

This chapter describes six alternative methods of computing the cost of a manufactured item. Variable costing, also know as direct costing, is contrasted with full absorption costing. Each method can be associated with actual, normal, and standard costing. This chapter provides a detailed comparison of four combinations using variable and full absorption costing with actual and normal costing. Since different decisions require specific inputs, the theme of the text, "different costs for different purposes" is highlighted.

CHAPTER HIGHLIGHTS

A. There is no single measure of costs appropriate for all decisions. Different costs are relevant for different purposes.

B. Managers must compute manufacturing costs based on **full absorption** costing principles for external reporting of the asset (inventory) and the expense (cost of goods sold). For external reporting, only full absorption costing conforms to GAAP. However, **variable costing** may be more appropriate for internal uses.

C. Cost inclusion refers to those costs which are to be **included** in the calculation of the per-unit manufacturing cost. The choices are identified as variable or full absorption cost.

D. Cost measure refers to how the costs are **measured**. The choices are actual, normal, or standard costs.

E. Regardless of the product costing method used, nonmanufacturing costs (marketing and adminstrative costs) are never included in the manufacturing cost of the product.

F. Under **variable costing** (also known as direct costing) only the variable manufacturing costs are considered to be product costs. Fixed manufacturing costs are treated as period costs and are charged directly to the income statement. No fixed costs are attached to the inventory. Unit costs are computed as:

$$UC = DM + DL + VOH$$

where UC = unit product cost
DM = direct materials per unit
DL = direct labor per unit
VOH = variable manufacturing overhead per unit

G. Under the absorption costing method, all manufacturing costs, whether direct or indirect, fixed or variable, are included in the product's cost. Unit costs are computed as:

$$UC = DM + DL + VOH + FOH/X$$

where UC = unit product cost
DM = direct materials per unit
DL = direct labor per unit
VOH = variable manufacturing overhead per unit
FOH = total fixed manufacturing costs per period
X = units produced during the period

Alternatively, total manufacturing costs can be computed by summing all manufacturing costs for the period and dividing by the number of units produced during that period.

H. The difference between full absorption costing and variable costing lies solely in the treatment of fixed manufacturing costs. Full absorption costing includes fixed overhead costs in the unit costs, variable costing not only excludes it, but treats it as a period cost. When there is no change in inventory the two methods yield the same operating profit.

I. In periods of increasing inventory, absorption costing will assign more cost to the inventory as a result of the treatment of fixed overhead as part of the asset cost. Thus, more costs are deferred in inventory as compared to variable costing. If more costs are deferred, fewer costs will be charged to the period. Hence, in times of inventory increases, full absorption costing will show a higher operating profit. As inventory levels decrease, the situation will reverse. Over the life of the enterprise, the two methods will show the same total operating profit.

J. In general, if the fixed manufacturing cost per unit is the same for each year, the difference in profits can be calculated by the fixed overhead cost per unit multiplied by the change in the number of units in inventory. If the fixed cost per unit differs between years, then the difference must be determined by the formula:

| Manufacturing costs | + Costs from beginning inventory | − Costs to ending inventory | = Manufacturing costs incurred expensed |

K. In addition to selecting a cost inclusion method, managers must choose a cost measure approach. The alternatives are **actual**, **normal**, and **standard costing**.

L. **Actual unit costs** reflect the traditional historic cost recorded in the financial accounting records and include actual direct materials, actual direct labor, and actual manufacturing overhead per unit. If manufacturing costs are accumulated during interim periods, it is possible for actual manufacturing overhead per unit to be substantially different from quarter to quarter or month to month.

M. **Normal unit costs** incorporate a constant amount of the overhead to each unit produced throughout the year. To calculate the normal amount of overhead that should be assigned to every unit produced, a predetermined overhead rate is used.

The **predetermined overhead rate** is calculated at the beginning of the annual period by dividing estimated manufacturing overhead for the entire year by the expected output for the year. As units are produced, the normal overhead rate per unit is added to the actual direct material and actual direct labor costs to compute the total cost of the unit. Normal costing assures the same per unit overhead throughout the year, regardless of month to month fluctuations in actual costs and activity levels.

N. Overhead rates can be derived using many different activity levels. Managers would choose the base that best correlates overhead costs with the product produced. Alternatively, multiple bases can be used.

O. Overhead costs are applied to production using four steps:

1. Select an activity base.
2. Estimate the amount of overhead and the level of activity for the period.
3. Compute the predetermined overhead rate.
4. Apply overhead to production.

P. The flow of costs through "T" accounts using full absorption costing:

```
        WORK IN PROCESS           FINISHED GOODS         COST OF GOODS SOLD
   D. Materials  | no. of----->       | no. of----->       |
   D. Labor      | units completed    | units sold         |
(a)Applied       | times              | times              |
   Variable      | unit cost          | unit cost          |
   Overhead      |                    |                    |
(b)Applied       |
   Fixed Overhead|


VARIABLE MANUFACTURING OVERHEAD              FIXED MANUFACTURING OVERHEAD
     Actual     | (a) Applied                   Actual    | Applied
                |     Variable                            |   Fixed
                |     Overhead                            |   Overhead
```

The differences between the actual and applied fixed and variable overhead are charged to an overhead adjustment account.

Q. The flow of costs through "T" accounts using variable costing:

WORK-IN-PROCESS		FINISHED GOODS	COST OF GOODS SOLD
D. Materials D. Labor (a) Applied Variable Overhead	no. of → units completed times variable unit cost	no. of → units sold times variable unit cost	

VARIABLE MANUFACTURING OVERHEAD		FIXED MANUFACTURING OVERHEAD	
actual	(a) Applied Variable Overhead	charges for actual overhead	

The difference between the actual and applied variable overhead is charged to a variable overhead adjustment account.

R. The variable overhead adjustment account and the fixed overhead adjustment account may be (1) closed to the cost of goods sold or (2) prorated between the cost of goods sold, ending inventory and work in process.

S. As a result of two cost inclusion methods and three cost measure approaches, it is possible to have six different unit costs for the same manufactured item. Of the four presented in detail in this chapter, the choice of which cost is best depends on the use of the information.

SELF-TEST AND PRACTICE EXERCISES

A. MATCHING

Match each of the following terms with its meaning.

Term	Meaning
___1. Actual overhead rate	a. Direct materials + direct labor + actual overhead/unit (must include fixed as well as variable).
___2. Unit cost using full absorption costing	b. Actual direct materials + actual direct labor + predetermined manufacturing overhead/unit.
___3. Predetermined overhead rate	c. Direct material + direct labor + variable overhead/unit.
___4. Unit cost using normal costing	d. Actual manufacturing overhead divided by actual activity.
___5. Unit cost using variable costing	e. Estimated annual manufacturing overhead divided by estimated annual activity.
___6. Actual costing	f. Actual direct materials + actual direct labor + actual manufacturing overhead.

B. DIFFERENCES BETWEEN VARIABLE AND FULL ABSORPTION COSTING

The Peters Company has the following data in its records for the month of January:

Direct materials	$ 4,500
Direct labor	$ 7,500
Variable manufacturing overhead	$ 1,500
Fixed manufacturing overhead	$ 6,000
Number of units produced	1,500 units

REQUIRED:

1. Determine the unit cost for inventory purposes under variable costing.

2. Determine the unit cost for inventory purposes under full absorption costing.

3. Why isn't variable costing used in financial reporting?

C. DIFFERENCES BETWEEN ACTUAL AND NORMAL COSTING

The Hardnose Company uses direct labor hours as the activity base for deriving a predetermined overhead rate. At the beginning of the year the company estimated the following manufacturing costs:

Estimated direct material (2 units of A @ $ .60) = $1.20/unit
Estimated direct labor (2 hours @ $4.00 per hour) = $8.00/unit
Estimated variable overhead (2 hours @ $2.50 per hour) = $5.00/unit
Estimated fixed overhead (total annual cost) $21,000
Estimated total annual production   10,000 units

At the end of the year, the company's records reflected the following actual results:

Actual direct material (2 units of A @ $ .65) = $1.30/unit
Actual direct labor (3 hours @ $4.00 per hour) = $12.00/unit
Actual variable overhead (3 hours @ $3.00 per hour) = $9.00/unit
Actual fixed overhead (total annual cost) $24,000
Actual total annual production   10,000 units

REQUIRED:

1. What is the actual fixed overhead rate per unit?

2. What is the full absorption cost per unit using actual costing?

3. What is the predetermined overhead rate per direct labor hour?

4. How much overhead is applied to each unit?

5. What is the full absorption cost per unit using normal costing?

D. FLOW OF COSTS USING FULL ABSORPTION COSTING

The Amoure Company has the following transactions during the year:

    a. Purchased materials, $15,000.
    b. Used materials, $12,000 (all direct).
    c. Incurred direct labor costs, $18,000.
    d. Manufacturing overhead costs incurred, $25,000.
    e. Cost of units completed, $50,000.
    f. Cost of goods sold, $43,000.

REQUIRED:

1. Post the above transactions to the following "T" accounts:

    Materials Inventory   Work-in-Process

    Finished Goods Inventory   Cost of Goods Sold

2. What is the ending balance of the following accounts?

    (a) Materials Inventory   _____

    (b) Work-in-Process   _____

    (c) Finished Goods   _____

E. VARIABLE VS. FULL ABSORPTION COSTING WHEN INVENTORY LEVELS CHANGE

Assume the following information:

Selling price per unit	$15
Sales, in units	750 units
Production	1,000 units
Manufacturing costs:	
Direct materials	$2/unit
Direct labor	$6/unit
Variable overhead	$1/unit
Fixed overhead	$2,000 per year
Marketing costs	
Variable	$1/unit
Fixed	$500 per year

REQUIRED:

1. What is the unit cost of goods sold under variable costing?

2. What is the total cost of goods sold under variable costing?

3. What is the total cost of goods sold under full absorption costing?

4. What is the operating profit under variable costing?

5. What is the operating profit under full absorption costing?

6. Reconcile the difference between the two methods.

7. What will happen next year if all the inventory is sold?

SOLUTIONS

A. MATCHING:

   1. d   2. a   3. e   4. b   5. c   6. f

B. DIFFERENCES BETWEEN VARIABLE AND ABSORPTION COSTING:

  1.   Direct materials $4,500
       Direct labor   7,500
       Variable overhead   1,500
 (a) Total variable costs $13,500

 (b) Number of units   1,500

      Cost/unit (a)/(b) $9/unit

  2.   Direct materials $4,500
       Direct labor   7,500
       Variable overhead   1,500
       Fixed overhead   6,000
 (a) Total costs $19,500

 (b) Number of units   1,500

      Cost/unit (a)/(b) $13/unit

  3. Historic cost principle requires that all costs necessary to bring an asset into its intended working condition become part of the asset cost. Since fixed manufacturing overhead is needed to produce the inventory, each unit must absorb the fixed cost.

C. DIFFERENCES BETWEEN ACTUAL AND NORMAL COSTING:

  1. $24,000/30,000 hours = $ .80/hour   or $2.40/unit

  2. $1.30 + $12.00 + $9.00 + $2.40 = $24.70/unit

  3. $21,000/20,000 hour = $1.05/hour

  4. Variable overhead applied is $7.50 (3 hrs. x $2.50/hr.)
     Fixed overhead applied is $3.15 (3 hrs. x $1.05/hr.)
     Total overhead applied is $10.65.

  5. $1.30 + $12.00 + $7.50 + $3.15 = $23.95/unit

D. FLOW OF COSTS USING FULL ABSORPTION/ACTUAL COSTING:

1. | Materials Inventory | | Work-in-Process | |
    |---|---|---|---|
    | (a) 15,000 | (b) 12,000 | (b) 12,000 | (e) 50,000 |
    | | | (c) 18,000 | |
    | | | (d) 25,000 | |

Finished Goods		Cost of Goods Sold	
(e) 50,000	(f) 43,000	(f) 43,000	

2. (a) $3,000 ($15,000 - $12,000)
   (b) $5,000 ($12,000 + $18,000 + $25,000 - $50,000)
   (c) $7,000 ($50,000 - $43,000).

E. VARIABLE VS. ABSORPTION COSTING WHEN INVENTORY LEVELS CHANGE:

1. $2 + $6 + $1 = $9 per unit

2. $9 x 750 units = $6,750

3. | | |
    |---|---|
    | Variable manufacturing costs | $6,750 |
    | Fixed manufacturing costs | 1,500 (750/1000 x $2,000) |
    | Total cost of goods sold | $8,250 |

    Alternatively, $11 x 750 units = $8,250.

4. | | | |
    |---|---|---|
    | Sales (750 units @ $15) | | $11,250 |
    | Less Variable costs: | | |
    | Manufacturing | $6,750 | |
    | Marketing (750 @ $1) | 750 | 7,500 |
    | Contribution margin | | $ 3,750 |
    | Less Fixed expenses | | |
    | Manufacturing | $2,000 | |
    | Marketing | 500 | 2,500 |
    | Operating profit | | $ 1,250 |

5. | | |
    |---|---|
    | Sales (see part 4) | $11,250 |
    | Less cost of goods sold (see part 3) | 8,250 |
    | Gross margin | $ 3,000 |
    | Less marketing expenses ($750 + $500) | 1,250 |
    | Operating profit | $ 1,750 |

6. The difference of $500 is due to the fixed manufacturing cost per unit of $2.00 ($2,000/1,000) attaching to the 250 units in ending inventory under full absorption costing and being deferred as an asset in the inventory account. Under variable costing, all the fixed overhead is charged to the period and none of it can be deferred.

7. The cost of goods sold under full absorption will be $500 higher because the company would be selling units that have a higher cost associated with them. The operating profits will be $500 lower using full absorption compared to variable costing.

STUDY PLAN

1. Review self-study problem number 1.

2. Do Exercise 14. Another way to answer part c is to determine the cost of goods sold and operating profit under each alternative. Try to resolve the difference this way:

(a) Under variable costing the manufacturing costs charged to the period would be:

Variable cost of goods sold ($48,000 + $36,000 + $12,000)	$96,000
Fixed manufacturing costs	12,000
Total costs charged under variable costing	$108,000

(b) Under full absorption costing, the manufacturing costs charged to the period would be:

Variable cost of goods sold (see above)	$96,000
Fixed cost of goods sold ($12,000/50,000 units times 48,000 units)	11,520
Total costs charged under full absorption	$107,520

(c) The difference between $108,000 and $107,520, or $480, can be explained by the fixed costs deferred under full absorption costing that is expensed under variable costing.

3. Review self-study problem 2.

4. Do exercise 22 part a. Answer these questions:

   (a) How would a company decide whether direct labor hours or direct labor costs should be the base to use? Answer: Whichever method best met the cost/benefit test; usually the method that more closely matched overhead costs actually associated with the products produced.

   (b) How have high-tech firms changed their costing systems? Answer: High-tech firms have moved away from direct labor hours as a base and changed to machine hours. In addition, direct labor can be classified as part of overhead when the direct labor costs are insignficant to the product.

5. Review the following outline. By now you should be able to compute four different inventory costs.

REVIEW OUTLINE

I. Accounting for inventories.

   A. Cost inclusion methods.

      1. Variable costing (also known as direct costing) includes direct materials, direct labor, and variable manufacturing overhead in the cost of goods sold. Fixed manufacturing costs are expensed during the period.

      2. Full absorption costing (or absorption costing) includes not only direct materials, direct labor and variable manufacturing overhead, but also fixed manufacturing overhead.

         a. It is the only method acceptable for financial reporting.

         b. In periods of rising inventory levels, full absorption costing will cause some of the fixed costs to be deferred to a future period and higher income will be reported in the current period as compared to variable costing.

         c. In periods of decreasing inventory levels, absorption costing will cause the fixed costs previously deferred to be charged against the current period and lower income will be reported as compared to variable costing.

   B. Cost measure approaches.

      1. Actual costing includes the actual amounts recognized in the books of the company.

2. Normal costing requires the company to estimate an overhead rate. This overhead rate is applied to the actual activity incurred during the period. Under normal costing, actual direct materials, and direct labor are part of inventory values.

3. Standard costing reflects estimates of efficiently used resources for direct materials, direct labor, and manufacturing overhead.

II. Overhead rates.

A. The purpose is to spread actual overhead costs evenly to the products produced throughout the entire period.

B. Many different bases are possible. Managers must select the one that best matches the cost with cost object.

III. Use of cost information.

A. There is no one best cost method. The costs of the system must be weighed against the system's benefits.

B. There is no one method appropriate for all decisions.

CHAPTER 4

ACCOUNTING FOR RESOURCE FLOWS: COST ACCUMULATION

This chapter shows how the accounting system records and reports the flow of resources in organizations. Manufacturing systems are examined in order to explain how the cost of a unit is determined for inventory purposes. The chapter provides a user-perspective of the way accounting systems record and report the flow of resources. Job and process costing is introduced. Standard costing is explained in more detail.

CHAPTER HIGHLIGHTS

A. Planning and performance evaluations in organizations are facilitated by organizational units set up along lines of responsibility. **Responsibility centers** are units in which clear-cut lines of responsibility are established and one or more managers are held responsible for the unit's activities. Examples of responsibility centers are divisions, territories, plants, and product lines.

B. Costs are accumulated by responsibility centers and then allocated to specific products for inventory valuation and managerial information.

C. In a manufacturing company, the **work-in-process** account serves two purposes: (1) it accounts for the inputs needed to make the product and (2) it describes the transformation of these inputs into a finished product. Normally, each department has a separate work-in-process account.

D. The three major cost components of a manufactured good are (1) **direct materials**, (2) **direct labor**, and (3) **manufacturing overhead**. Direct labor and overhead are **conversion costs**.

E. The accounting system has two purposes in manufacturing companies: (1) to accumulate costs and (2) to allocate costs.

F. The first step in the manufacturing process is to buy materials. When materials are purchased, the accounting entry records an increase in the asset called materials inventory and its related liability called accounts payable.

G. As materials are requisitioned, materials classified as direct are charged (debited) to the work-in-process account. Indirect materials are charged to variable manufacturing overhead. Regardless of the classification of the material, the materials inventory account is reduced (credited).

H. As labor costs are incurred, direct labor is charged to the work-in-process account and indirect labor is charged to variable or fixed manufacturing overhead (depending on the nature of the expense).

I. Manufacturing overhead costs are charged to work-in-process. Thus, WIP includes direct materials, direct labor, and overhead.

J. As goods are completed, they are physically transferred to the finished goods storeroom. The cost of the units completed during the current period is referred to as the cost of goods manufactured.

K. When a sale is made, the revenue is recognized. In addition, the cost of the sale is recorded by charging the **cost of goods sold** with the manufacturing cost and reducing the finished goods inventory by the same amount.

L. Regardless of the cost accumulation system, the matching concept in accounting requires that only the cost of resources consumed during the period are charged to the period. Costs that represent future benefits to the company must be deferred as an asset. The basic accounting formula incorporates the matching concept because beginning inventory is conceptually used up during the period and ending inventory is still considered an asset (unexpired cost). Thus, to compute the cost of materials used during the period, the cost of goods manufactured, and the cost of goods sold, the general formula is:

Beginning inventory + Transfers in - Transfers out = Ending Inventory

where the materials used, the cost of goods manufactured, and the cost of goods sold are all considered transfers out of the accounts.

M. More specifically, to compute the cost of goods manufactured, use the formula:

Beginning WIP + Direct + Direct + Overhead - Ending WIP = Cost of
Inventory   Materials Labor   Inventory   Goods
                                                        Manufactured

and to compute the cost of goods sold, use the formula:

Beginning FG + Cost of Goods - Ending FG = Cost of Goods Sold
Inventory   Manufactured   Inventory

N. There are two major types of production operations: **job and process**. In job costing, costs are collected for each "unit" produced. In process costing costs are accumulated in a department or production process during an accounting period, then the costs are spread evenly over the unit produced during that period.

O. To record the flow of costs for job costing, a separate WIP account is set up for each job ("unit"). To record the flow of costs for process costing, a separate WIP account is set up for each department or process.

39

P. The costs of record-keeping are usually higher for job costing than process costing. However, a job system usually generates more accurate unit costs for non-homogeneous units.

Q. High tech firms have found that direct labor, which is not a substantial input cost to some products, can be combined with overhead and still provide useful cost information.

R. When standard costs are used, the cost of a unit includes only the standard amount for materials, labor, and overhead.

S. Standard costs may be useful to managers -- alone or in combination with a standard cost system. When a standard cost system is used, the difference between the actual and standard cost is called a variance and it is written off in the period incurred.

T. Merchandise companies do not require detailed cost systems for inventory.

U. Service organizations, which have no substantial inventory, could use a standard cost system to accumulate costs for each job.

SELF-TEST AND PRACTICE EXERCISES

A. MATCHING

Match each of the following terms with its meaning.

<u>Term</u>

___1. Cost of goods sold for a manufacturing company

___2. Cost of goods manufactured

___3. Standard costs

___4. Variance adjustment account

___5. Materials used

___6. Job costing

___7. Process costing

<u>Meaning</u>

a. Accumulates costs by units.

b. Beginning materials inventory plus purchases less ending materials inventory.

c. Accumulates costs by the department of process.

d. Beginning finished goods inventory plus cost of goods manufactured less ending finished goods inventory.

e. Uses an efficient cost for materials, labor, and overhead.

f. Beginning WIP + Direct Materials + Direct Labor + Overhead - Ending WIP.

g. Used when actual costs differ from standard costs.

B. DIFFERENCE BETWEEN NORMAL AND STANDARD COSTING

The Hardnose Company, in Chapter 3, Exercise C, developed the following standards for their product:

Standard direct material (2 units of A @ $ .50) = $1.00/unit
Standard direct labor (2 hours @ $4.00 per hour)= $8.00/unit
Standard variable overhead (2 hours @ $2.25 per hour)= $4.50/unit

REQUIRED: (You must refer back to Exercise C in Chapter 3.)

1. What is the predetermined fixed overhead rate per hour?

2. What is the standard fixed overhead cost per unit?

3. What is the normal fixed overhead cost per unit?

4. What is the variable standard unit cost?

5. What is the full absorption standard unit cost?

6. What is the variable normal cost?

C. USING THE ACCOUNTING EQUATION

Assume the following facts:

Beginning materials inventory	$30
Beginning work-in-process inventory	26
Beginning finished goods inventory	50
Direct materials requisitioned	80
Direct labor	35
Manufacturing overhead (including $2 of indirect materials)	16
Ending materials inventory	34
Ending work-in-process inventory	23
Ending finished goods inventory	55

REQUIRED:

1. Determine the amount of materials purchased during the period.

2. Determine the cost of goods manufactured during the period.

3. Determine the cost of goods sold during the period.

D. JOB COSTING FOR A MANUFACTURING COMPANY

The Wisher Products Company uses a job costing system. The company estimated its annual overhead to be $50,000, and the number of direct labor hours for the year to be 10,000 hours. In the first month, the following jobs were completed:

	Job #1	Job #2
Direct materials used	$1,000	$1,500
Direct labor cost	$2,000	$2,500
Direct labor hours	1,000 hours	1,200 hours

REQUIRED:

1. What is the company's predetermined overhead rate using direct labor hours as the base?

2. What is the overhead assigned to job #1?

3. What is the overhead assigned to job #2?

4. What is the total manufacturing cost of job #1?

5. What is the total manufacturing cost of job #2?

E. PROCESS COSTING

Assume the company in Exercise D used a process system. The following costs were accumulated by departments:

	Dept. A	Dept. B
Direct materials used	$2,000	$ 500
Direct labor cost	$3,000	$1,500
Direct labor hours	1,500 hours	700 hours

REQUIRED:

1. What is the company's predetermined overhead rate?

2. What are the overhead costs charged to Dept. A?

3. What are the total costs accumulated in Dept. A?

4. What are the overhead costs charged to Dept. B?

5. What are the total costs accumulated in Dept. B?

6. What are the unit costs associated with the two jobs?

7. In this case, which costing system provides a finer cost for job #1 and job #2.

SOLUTIONS

A. MATCHING:

    1. d   2. f   3. e   4. g   5. b   6. a   7. c

B. DIFFERENCES BETWEEN NORMAL AND STANDARD COSTING:

    1. $21,000/20,000 direct labor hours = $1.05/direct labor hour.

    2. $1.05/direct labor hour @ 2 standard hours = $2.10/unit

    3. $1.05/direct labor hour @ 3 actual hours = $3.15/unit

    4. $1.00 + $8.00 + $4.50 = $13.50

    5. $1.00 + $8.00 + $4.50 + $2.10 = $15.60

    6. $1.30 + $12.00 + $7.50 = $20.80

C. USING THE ACCOUNTING EQUATION:

    1. $86 [30 + X - (80 + 2) = 34]

    2. $134 (26 + 80 + 35 + 16 - 23)

    3. $129 (50 + 134 - 55)

D. JOB COSTING FOR A MANUFACTURING COMPANY

    1. $50,000/10,000 hours = $5/direct labor hour

    2. 1,000 hours @ $5 per hour = $5,000

    3. 1,200 hours @ $5 per hour = $6,000

    4. $1,000 + $2,000 + $5,000 = $8,000

    5. $1,500 + $2,500 + $6,000 = $10,000

E. PROCESS COSTING

1. $50,000/10,000$ hours = $5/direct labor hour
   This is the same as Exercise D part 1.

2. 1,500 hours @ $5 per hour = $7,500

3. $2,000 + $3,000 + $7,500 = $12,500

4. 700 hours @ $5 per hour = $3,500

5. $500 + $1,500 + $3,500 = $5,500

6. [Dept A + Dept B]/2 jobs

   [$12,500 + $5,500]/2 = $9,000 per job

7. Job costing reflects Job #1's cost as $8,000 while Job #2's cost as $10,000. However, the process system spreads the $18,000 cost evenly over the two jobs and determines an average cost of $9,000 each. Thus, the job system presents finer, and more accurate, information.

STUDY PLAN

1. Review Exhibits 4.2, 4.3, and 4.4. You should now be able to prepare an income statement for a manufacturing company (like Exhibit 4.6).

2. Try Exercise 12. Answer the following additional questions:

   (a) What is the amount of under- or overapplied overhead? Answer: There is $10,000 of overhead incurred which is not yet charged to production, and accordingly is called underapplied. It would be transferred to the variance adjustment account.

   (b) How would the underapplied overhead be disposed of at the end of the accounting period for external reporting? Answer: It would either be charged directly to the cost of goods sold or it could be pro-rated between the work-in-process, finished goods, and cost of goods sold.

3. Review problem for self-study number 2. Why did the company use job costing instead of process costing?

4. Review problem for self-study number 3. How does the income statement in part (a) differ from the income statement in Exhibit 4.6?

REVIEW OUTLINE

I. Cost accumulation and cost allocation.

   A. Normally, costs are initially accumulated in responsibility centers (e.g., divisions, territories, plants, product lines, departments).

   B. To provide product cost information, costs must be allocated from responsibility centers to products.

II. Components of product cost.

   A. According to generally accepted accounting principles, product cost is composed of direct materials, direct labor, and manufacturing overhead.

   B. While only full absorption costing is acceptable for financial reporting, managers often find variable costing helpful for planning and decision making.

   C. Regardless of the approach, a company may use actual, normal, or standard costing.

III. Flow of manufacturing costs.

   A. Raw materials that have not yet entered the production process are held in the raw materials storeroom. As they are requisitioned, they are classified as either direct or indirect materials.

   B. Costs of unfinished goods in production in the factory are accumulated in the work-in-process inventory accounts. These costs are direct materials, direct labor, and manufacturing overhead.

   C. Costs of unsold finished goods, normally held in the finished goods storeroom, are accumulated in the finished goods inventory account.

   D. At the time the goods are sold, costs are transferred from the finished goods inventory account to the cost of goods sold account.

IV. Allocation of manufacturing costs to products.

   A. Direct materials and direct labor usually need no allocation to products.

   B. Manufacturing overhead is more difficult to trace down to products.

      1. Procedure for allocating manufacturing overhead to products under an actual cost system requires waiting until the end of a period when

all the costs are known. Then, using some activity (such as units or direct hours) the actual costs are allocated to the units produced.

    2. Procedure for allocating manufacturing overhead to products under a normal cost system requires estimating fixed and variable costs for the coming period. In addition, the company must estimate the level of activity (in terms of direct labor hours, units to be produced, etc.) for the coming period. This gives the predetermined overhead rate calculated as follows:

$$\text{Predetermined overhead rate} = \frac{\text{Estimated total manufacturing overhead}}{\text{Estimated total activity}}$$

The rate is used throughout the period to apply manufacturing overhead to the products produced.

    3. Procedure for allocating manufacturing overhead to products under a standard cost system is the same as a normal cost system except that the rate is applied only to the standard amount of inputs allowed for the product.

  C. Under normal or standard cost systems, variances will exist at the end of an accounting period. These variances may be expensed to the period or prorated to the affected accounts.

V. The basic accounting equation.

The basic accounting equation is valid throughout the system:

$$BB + TI = TO + EB$$

where BB = Beginning balance
      TI = Transfers in
      TO = Transfers out
      EB = Ending balance

VI. Job and process costing.

  A. Job costing accumulates costs by a job. Separate work-in-process accounts exist for each job in the accounting system.

  B. Process costing accumulates costs by a department or process. Each department or process has a work-in-process account. Costs per unit are determined by adding all costs for a period and spreading these costs over the units produced during the period.

CHAPTER 5

COST ALLOCATION

This chapter discusses cost allocation to products, departments, and divisions. The rationale for cost allocations is presented, cost accounting methods are demonstrated, and problems associated with cost allocation in decision making are highlighted.

CHAPTER OUTLINE

A. Accounting distinguishes between a direct cost and a common cost. A direct cost can be identified specifically with, or traced directly to a cost object. It needs no allocation. A **common cost** results from the joint use of a facility by several products, departments, or processes. It must be allocated to a cost object.

B. Common cost allocations must be made for inventory valuation in external financial reports. However, for decision-making purposes they are often misleading.

C. Managers have several reasons for allocating costs, for example: (1) it puts users on notice that common costs must be covered by departments and (2) it encourages users not to overuse common facilities.

D. The cost allocation process involves three steps: (1) accumulating costs; (2) identifying the recipient of the allocated costs; and (3) selecting a basis for allocating the accumulated costs to the recipient.

E. In general, the allocation of costs should follow a logical format. First allocate costs associated directly with departments, next, allocate costs not associated with departments, and finally allocate all service department costs to the production departments. In steps two and three, it is necessary to select an allocation base. In doing so managers must seek a logical relation between costs and the allocation and if none exist, they must then allocate on an arbitrary basis.

F. The **step allocation process** is often used to allocate costs from service departments to production departments. This procedure starts by allocating one service department's costs to production departments and to all other service departments; then a second service department's costs are allocated to production departments and all other service departments except the first one. An alternative to the step allocation method is the reciprocal method.

F. A cost allocation problem arises when more than one product emerges from a single production process. The common cost is called a **joint product** cost. Costs incurred after the split off point are called **additional processing** costs. To determine the costs of the finished products, an allocation of the joint cost is necessary. Two methods are commonly used: the **net realizable method** (also known as the relative sales value method) and the **physical units** method. The physical units method allocates costs according to a physical measure such as pounds or units. The net realizable value method allocates joint costs in proportion to the net realizable value of the joint products at the split-off point. If information about selling prices cannot be determined, the **approximate net realizable value** method can be used.

G. A by-product is similar to a joint product but it is of nominal value. By-products are often valued at their **net realizable value**.

H. Marketing and administrative expenses are allocated using similar techniques as those used in manufacturing cost analysis.

SELF-TEST AND PRACTICE EXERCISES

A. **MATCHING**

Match each of the following terms with its meaning.

<u>Term</u>

<u>Meaning</u>

___1. Common cost

a. Selecting a method or basis for relating various accumulated costs with the respective recipients.

___2. Direct cost

b. The point where all costs are no longer joint costs but can be identified with individual products.

___3. Allocation base

c. Method of allocating costs according to some physical measure.

___4. Service department

d. One of two or more outputs from a process that must be produced or acquired simultaneously

___5. Joint product

e. Cost resulting from use of a facility, or a service that benefits several products or departments and must be allocated accordingly.

___6. By-product

f. A department that provides services to other departments, rather than direct work on salable product.

___7. Split-off point

g. A method for allocating joint costs in proportion to net realizable value of the joint products.

___8. Net realizable value method

h. Selling price of an item less reasonable further costs to make the item ready for sale and to sell it.

___9. Physical units method

i. Cost that can be directly attributed to a product or department.

___10. Approximate net realizable value

j. A joint product whose value is so small in relation to the value of the other joint products that it does not receive normal accounting treatment.

B. STEP ALLOCATION PROCEDURE

From the following data for the ABC Corporation, use the step method to prepare a schedule showing the reallocation of overhead costs to production departments.

	Service Departments			Production Departments		
	1	2	3	4	5	6
Overhead costs before reallocation	300	210	240	160	110	105
Proportions of service to be furnished by:						
Dept. 1 to other depts.	-	10%	20%	30%	15%	25%
Dept. 2 to other depts.	20%	-	10%	30%	10%	30%
Dept. 3 to other depts.	-	10%	-	30%	30%	30%

C. ALLOCATING TO UNITS PRODUCED

In Exercise B, Producing Department 4 manufactured 100 units.

REQUIRED:

1. What would be the overhead cost per unit for inventory purposes?

2. How much of Service Department 1's cost is in every finished product manufactured by producing Department 4?

3. If Producing Department 6 was dropped, what would be the effect on Producing Departments 4 & 5?

D. ALLOCATING COSTS TO JOINT PRODUCTS

Products P and Q are joint products for which joint production costs incurred during June 1985 were $300,000. Both products are sold in their split-off condition. June sales were 30,000 units of product P and 50,000 units of product Q. Product Q sells for $6 per unit and P sells for $4.50. Ending inventory consisted of 10,000 units of P and 10,000 units of Q.

REQUIRED:

1. Prepare a schedule showing the allocation of costs to the cost of goods sold and inventories using the physical units method.

	Units sold	Ending inventory	Total units	Percentage of total cost	Allocation of total cost	Cost per unit
P	_____	_____	____	_____	_____	____
Q	_____	_____	____	_____	_____	____

	Cost of goods sold	Ending inventory	Total mfg. cost
P	_____	_____	_____
Q	_____	_____	_____

2. Prepare a schedule showing the allocation of costs to the cost of goods sold and ending inventories using the relative sales value method.

Product	Units produced	Selling price	Sales value	Allocation ratio	Cost allocation	Cost per unit
P	_____	_____	_____	_____	_____	_____
Q	_____	_____	_____	_____	_____	_____

	Cost of goods sold	Ending inventory	Total mfg. cost
P	_____	_____	_____
Q	_____	_____	_____

3. Product Q can be processed further at a cost of $1.00 per unit. If it is processed further, the unit can be sold for $7.50. Should product Q be processed further? Which allocation method should the manager use in making the decision?

SOLUTIONS

A. MATCHING:

1. e   2. i   3. a   4. f   5. d

6. j   7. b   8. g   9. c   10. h

B. STEP ALLOCATION PROCEDURE:

	Service Departments			Production Departments		
	1	2	3	4	5	6
Overhead costs before reallocation	300	210	240	160	110	105
Proportions of service to be furnished by:						
Dept. 1 to other depts.	(300)	30	60	90	45	75
Dept. 2 to other depts.		(240)	30	90	30	90
Dept. 3 to other depts.			(330)	110	110	110
Total overhead of production departments				450	295	380

C. ALLOCATING TO UNITS PRODUCED:

1. $4.50

2. .90 allocated from dept. 1 directly to dept. 4 (90/100)
   .11 allocated from dept. 1 through dept. 2 [(30/240) x 90]/100
   .20 allocated from dept. 1 through dept. 3 [(60/330) x 110]/100
   $1.21

3. If one producing department was dropped, the remaining producing departments would have to bear a greater burden of overhead expenses.

D. ALLOCATING COSTS TO JOINT PRODUCTS:

1.

	Units sold	Ending inventory	Total units	Percentage of total cost	Allocation of total cost	Cost per unit
P	30,000	10,000	40,000	40%	120,000	$3
Q	50,000	10,000	60,000	60%	180,000	$3
			100,000	100%	300,000	

	Cost of goods sold	Ending inventory	Total
P	90,000	30,000	120,000
Q	150,000	30,000	180,000

2.

Product	Units produced	Selling price	Sales value	Allocation ratio	Cost allocation	Cost per unit
P	40,000	$4.50	$180,000	18/54 = 1/3	100,000	2.500
Q	60,000	$6.00	$360,000	36/54 = 2/3	200,000	3.333

	Cost of goods sold	Ending inventory	Total
P	75,000	25,000	100,000
Q	166,667	33,333	200,000

3. Yes. Product Q should not be processed further because the incremental revenues of $1.50 more than offset the incremental costs of $1.00 per unit. The company would be better off by $30,000 ($.50 x 60,000 units) when all the units are sold.

The allocation method is irrelevant to this business decision. The allocation method only affects the way the transaction will be reported in the external reports if inventory exists at the end of the period.

STUDY PLAN

1. The study guide exercises are like Exercises 14, 16, 20, and 24. Try these exercises next.

2. Review the principles of cost allocation on page 164 of the text. Then try a more challenging problem that requires your analysis of the allocation system (like problem 34).

3. Review the following outline.

REVIEW OUTLINE

I. The nature of common costs.

    A. Common costs are not directly identified with one department, product or process, but results from the joint use of a facility.

    B. For external reporting purposes, allocating costs is often necessary in valuing assets such as inventory.

    C. Common cost allocations in managerial reporting often lead to misleading conclusions.

II. General principles of cost allocation.

    A. The cost allocation process involves three steps.

        1. Accumulating costs.
        2. Identifying the recipient of the allocated costs.
        3. Selecting a basis for allocating the accumulated costs to the recipient.

    B. Guidelines for selecting the basis of allocation.

        1. Examine past cost behavior to find a relationship between costs and an allocation base.
        2. Evaluate operations to find a logical relation between costs and an allocation base.
        3. If costs can only be allocated on an arbitrary basis, an evaluation should be made to determine whether the costs really have to be allocated at all.

III. Cost allocation procedures.

    A. Manufacturing overhead allocation.

        1. Manufacturing overhead is first allocated to all production and service departments for cost control purposes.

        2. Steps in cost allocation.

            a. Costs that can be directly linked with departments are allocated first.
            b. Costs that are related to a department's activity, but cannot be directly attributed to the department are allocated on a basis that makes sense, but is necessarily arbitrary.

B. Service department cost allocation.

   1. After costs have been allocated to all departments for control purposes, they are allocated from service departments to production departments and finally to units produced for product costing.

   2. Steps in cost allocation.

      a. When departments service only production departments, allocate costs on a logical basis.

      b. When departments service other service departments as well as production departments, one method of allocating costs is the step-down allocation procedure. Using the step-down method, the costs of the department which receives the smallest dollar amount of service from other service departments is allocated first; the department receiving the next least service from the other service departments is allocated next, and so on. After a service department's costs have been distributed, no costs are allocated to it.

C. Joint products.

   1. When more than one product is created from a production process, the common costs must be allocated for inventory purposes.

   2. Joint costs are costs of the process that are incurred prior to the split-off point of separable products.

   3. Two methods of allocating these costs are commonly used.

      a. Net realizable value or approximate net realizable value method.
      b. Physical units measure.

D. By-products.

   1. These occur in a manufacturing process similar to joint products but are of nominal value.

   2. By-products are often valued at net realizable value at the split-off point.

E. Marketing and administrative expense.

   1. Not required for inventory costing, therefore it is less likely to be found in managerial reports.

   2. Allocated to bring managers' attention to the full cost of producing and selling the product.

CHAPTER 6

ESTIMATING COST BEHAVIOR

Managerial accounting information serves two major purposes: (1) managerial decision making and (2) managerial planning. This is the first of four chapters that focuses on accounting for decision making. In this chapter, the concepts of fixed and variable costs are utilized in estimating the expected costs of a particular action. Various methods are presented, including the engineering method and regression analysis, which are useful to managers in predicting future costs.

CHAPTER HIGHLIGHTS

A. Conceptually, all costs are classified as fixed or variable. **Variable costs** are costs that change as the level of activity changes (although they are constant per unit). **Fixed costs** do not change as activity level changes (but unit costs change). The definition of fixed cost assumes a short-run orientation and a **specified relevant** range. Total production capacity can only be changed in the long run.

B. The **relevant range** is also an important concept in estimating cost behavior. The relevant range is the level of activity likely to be undertaken with the existing plant.

C. The total costs for a time period is the sum of the fixed costs and the variable costs. The total variable costs are determined by multiplying the variable cost per unit (the variable rate) by the number of units of activity.

D. Practically, many costs cannot be neatly identified as purely fixed or only variable. Therefore, statistical and other techniques for estimating cost behavior are needed.

E. Cost estimation methods try to utilize the equation total costs equal total variable costs plus fixed costs. In this equation, total variable costs is a function of the variable rate per unit multiplied by some independent variable (often number of units). The equation is written as $TC = F + VX$.

F. Costs classified as fixed fall into two categories: capacity and discretionary. **Capacity costs** provide a firm with the facilities to produce or to sell or both. **Discretionary costs** are not necessary in the short run to operate a business, but are essential for achieving long-term goals. An example of a discretionary cost is research cost.

G. Perfectly straight fixed and variable cost behavior patterns are not always found in practice. **Curvilinear** costs vary with volume but not proportionally. Often this occurs as a result of learning acquired from experience in making the product. Some costs have fixed and variable components such as utility cost. These costs are called **semivariable** or mixed.

Other costs are fixed over a small activity range and must increase in amount at designated intervals. These costs are called **semifixed** or step costs. The number of computer operators needed to process input forms is an example of a semifixed cost.

H. There is often systematic learning from experience. **Learning curves** reflect the phenomenon that is found when the cost to complete a unit is reduced as productivity increases. The possible effect of learning on cost is important for decision making and performance evaluation.

I. The major purpose of cost estimation is to divide total cost into its fixed and variable cost components so predictions can be made. The following expression reflects the basic cost relationship:

$$TC = F + VX$$

where: TC = total costs
F = fixed costs
V = variable rate per unit
X = units of activity

J. Time and motion studies performed by engineers indicate what cost should be. The **engineering method** of estimating costs is most useful when input/output relationships are well defined and stable over time.

K. Another approach to estimating costs is called **account analysis**. Each element in the chart of accounts is labeled either fixed or variable. Historic records are examined to generate the total fixed costs and variable rate of the period.

L. Cost behavior of a firm often follows a specific trend. Using past data, future costs can be estimated. This technique allows for adjustments for inflation as well as changes in the relationship between costs and activity. For example, a prior period fixed cost may be changed to the variable cost category based on expected conditions.

Steps taken to analyze historic data include: (1) **review alternative activity bases** (the independent variable), (2) **plot the data**, (3) **examine the data and method of accumulation**.

M. One common method of separating costs into their fixed and variable components is visual curve fitting. **Visual curve fitting** requires the analyst to manually draw a predictor line through data points that seems to capture the trend. A variation of visual curve fitting is the **high-low method**, which draws a predictor line based on two representative points. The technique utilizes the point-slope formula, where the change in the dependent variable divided by the change in the independent variable is called the variable rate (or slope). The fixed costs are determined by the line's Y-intercept.

N. A more sophisticated approach to predicting costs uses statistical analysis called **regression analysis**. This technique fits a trend line through data points using a process called the method of least squares. The method, based on statistical assumption, results in a line that not only helps predict costs but also gives the standard error of the coefficient and the R-squared. However, the method does require a good understanding of the underlying assumptions, and an analyst should be trained in the technique before applying it in practice.

SELF-TEST AND PRACTICE EXERCISES

A. MATCHING

Match each of the following terms with its meaning.

Term	Meaning
___1. Learning curve effect	a. Fixed costs that are not necessary in the short run.
___2. Semi-fixed costs	b. Costs that increase in steps.
___3. Account analysis	c. Costs that have both fixed and variable components.
___4. Visual curve fitting.	d. Review of each account and classification of the account according to the cost behavior.
___5. Discretionary costs	e. Fits a line through data points using the method of least squares.
___6. Semivariable costs	f. Fits a line through data points using two representative points.
___7. High-low method	g. Fits a line through data points manually.
___8. Engineering method	h. A constant percentage reduction in the average cost as a result of experience.
___9. Relevant range	i. Indicates what costs should be as a result of time and motion studies.
___10. Regression analysis	j. The range of activity in which cost relationships are valid.

B. GRAPHING COST BEHAVIOR PATTERNS

Describe the cost behavior pattern reflected in the following graphs:

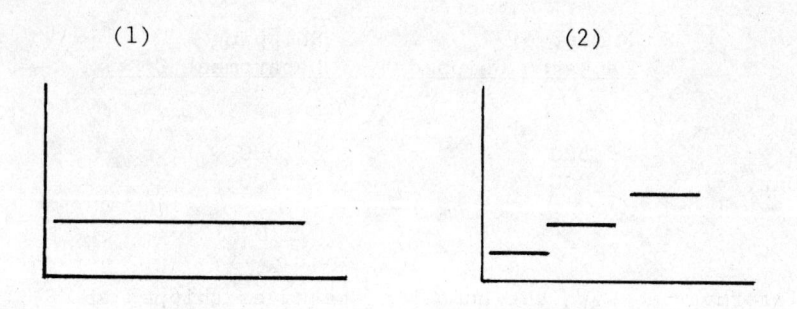

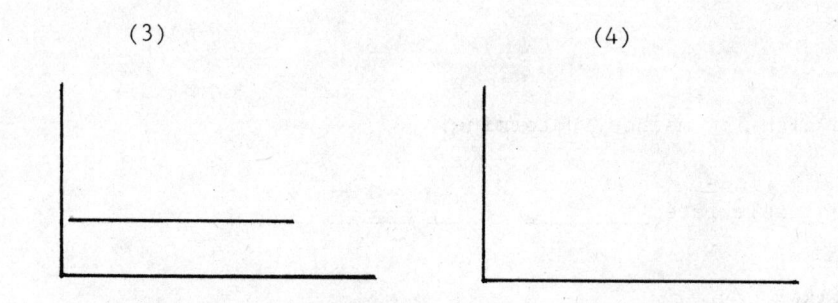

(1)

(2)

(3)

(4)

C. USING THE HIGH-LOW METHOD

Data from the shipping department of Weston Company for the first two months are as follows:

	Number of Packages Shipped	Shipping Department Costs
January	3,500	$5,000
February	4,000	5,500

REQUIRED:

1. Graph the information using the number of packages shipped as the independent variable.

2. Using the high-low method, determine:

   (a) the variable rate _____

   (b) the fixed cost _____

3. What is the formula for estimating total costs?

4. How does the concept of relevant range affect your prediction of future costs?

D. **INTERPRETING REGRESSION RESULTS**

The following output of overhead on direct labor hours was obtained using regression analysis:

Equation:

Intercept	$10,000
Slope	5

Statistical data:

Correlation coefficient	.89
R-square	.79

The company is planning on operating at a level that would call for 3,000 direct labor hours to be utilized for the coming year.

REQUIRED:

1. Use the regression output to write the overhead cost equation.

2. Based on the equation, compute the estimated overhead cost for the coming year.

3. What benefits does regression have over the high-low method?

SOLUTIONS

A. MATCHING:

    1. h   2. b   3. d   4. g   5. a
    6. c   7. f   8. i   9. j   10. e

B. GRAPHING COST BEHAVIOR PATTERNS:

    1. mixed or semivariable
    2. semifixed or step
    3. fixed
    4. variable

C. USING THE HIGH-LOW METHOD:

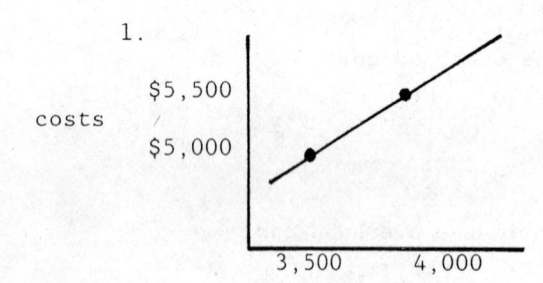

    1.

costs — graph with points at (3,500, $5,000) and (4,000, $5,500); x-axis: number of packages shipped

    2. (a) variable rate = $\dfrac{\text{change in dependent variable}}{\text{change in independent variable}}$

$$= \dfrac{5{,}500 - 5{,}000}{4{,}000 - 3{,}500} = \dfrac{500}{500} = \$1/\text{unit shipped}$$

    (b) Total costs = fixed costs + variable costs
         TC = FC + (VR)(X)

    using the higher point:

        $5,500 = FC + ($1/unit shipped)(4,000 units)
        $5,500 = FC + $4,000
        $1,500 = FC

using the lower point:

$$\$5,000 = FC + (\$1/\text{unit shipped})(3,500 \text{ units})$$
$$\$5,000 = FC + \$3,500$$
$$\$1,500 = FC$$

Therefore, fixed costs are $1,500.

3. TC = $1,500 + ($1/unit shipped)(number of units shipped)

4. Outside this range, the formula may not be valid.

D. INTERPRETING REGRESSION RESULTS:

1. TC = $10,000 + $5(Direct labor hours)

2. TC = $10,000 + $5(3,000)
   = $25,000

3. High-low only uses two representative points to estimate the relationship between costs and activity. Regression analysis incorporates all observations in the data set.

STUDY PLAN

1. Do Exercise 15 in the text. The problem is an extension of the study guide problem. Then try to do exercise 14 which integrates your knowledge of the way fixed and variable costs behave when predicting costs in the event of changes in activity levels.

2. Do Exercise 16 in the text. Can you explain why the variable rate would be different if only June and July data were available?

3. Do Exercise 23. Visual curve fitting can efficiently capture much of the underlying cost relationships without a lot of expense incurred by the firm.

4. Sometimes, the company needs better information about the cost structure. Regression is a technique that provides that information. As the manager, it is important that you know how to interpret the results of this statistical method. Do Exercises 21 and 22 to help you understand the output of a regression program.

REVIEW OUTLINE

I. The nature of fixed and variable costs.

   A. Short run vs. long run.

      1. The short run is a time period long enough to allow management to change the level of production or other activity within the constraints of current total capacity, usually a year.

      2. In the short run, costs that vary with activity levels are variable costs. Costs that do not vary are called fixed costs.

   B. Types of fixed costs.

      1. Capacity costs are costs incurred to provide the firm with the capacity to produce or sell or both (e.g., rent, depreciation).

      2. Discretionary costs are often incurred for purposes beyond those necessary for the current period (e.g., research, advertising).

II. Cost estimation.

   A. Cost estimation facilitates estimating the variable and fixed components of various types of costs. Total cost at any time can be expressed as the fixed cost for the period plus total variable costs (the variable rate times the units of activity).

   B. Methods of cost estimation.

      1. Account analysis.

      2. Engineering method.

      3. Estimating costs using historic data.

III. Steps in analyzing historical cost data.

   A. Review alternative activity bases (independent variable).

   B. Plot the data.

   C. Examine the data and the method of accumulation.

   D. Check for learning curve effect as well as other possible changes (such as technology, change in labor force).

IV. Methods of cost estimation using historic data.

   A. Visual curve fitting.

   B. High-low method.

   C. Regression analysis.

      1. Uses the least squares method.

      2. Generates the standard error of the regression coefficients.

      3. Generates the R-square.

      4. Several problems arise if assumptions are violated (multicollinearity, autocorrelation, and heteroscedasticity).

      5. Needs a trained statistician to avoid misinterpretations.

CHAPTER 7

COST-VOLUME-PROFIT ANALYSIS

The C-V-P model is the underlying model of a firm. This chapter explains the model and its limitations as well as its applications to business decision making. In general, we assume that short-run decisions are made within the constraints of plant capacity.

CHAPTER HIGHLIGHTS

A. A **model** is a simple representation of a complex set of relationships. It is essential for managers to understand the relationship among selling prices, unit costs, the volume sold, and profit. Virtually all financial decisions affect costs, volume, or profits.

B. Since operating profit is determined by subtracting total costs from total revenues, the **cost-volume-profit** equation is described as:

$$\text{Operating Profits } (\pi) = \text{Total Revenues} - \text{Total Costs}$$

or

$$\pi = PX - (VX + F)$$

where,

   P = unit selling price
   X = number of units sold
   V = unit variable costs
   F = fixed operating costs for the period

C. Profits calculated using the C-V-P model most probably will differ from net income reported using generally accepted accounting principles (GAAP). The C-V-P model reflects variable costing, while GAAP requires the full absorption method.

D. The contribution concept is particularly important in understanding the C-V-P model. The **contribution margin per unit** is the selling price per unit less the unit's variable costs. (The total contribution margin is determined by total sales revenues less total variable costs.)

The contribution margin represents what is left over from a sale after the variable costs of the sale are considered. The contribution margin conceptually covers fixed costs first, then contributes to the profitability of the company.

E. The **breakeven point** is the point where total costs and total revenues are equal. At sales activity below this point, the firm will incur a loss. At sales activity above this point, the firm will generate a profit. To determine the breakeven point, substitute zero for the profit figure in the cost-volume-profit equation. Thus, the breakeven point (X) is calculated using this equation:

$$0 = PX - (VX + F)$$

F. The breakeven equation derived from the cost-volume-profit model is best expressed in a formula format. The **breakeven point** can be determined by dividing fixed costs per period by the contribution margin per unit.

G. The breakeven formula can be adapted to assist managers in setting volumes that will generate a specific target profit. To modify the formula, treat a target profit as a fixed cost and include it in the numerator of the equation as follows:

$$\text{Volume to earn a specified target profit (lump-sum)} = \frac{\text{Fixed Costs + Target Profit}}{\text{Contribution Margin per Unit}}$$

If the target profit is a percentage of sales, rather than a lump-sum amount, the formula can be modified by treating the desired profit as a "variable cost". The above formula should be modified as follows:

$$\text{Volume to earn a specified profit (\% of sales)} = \frac{\text{Fixed Costs}}{\text{Contribution Margin per unit less (target percentage} \times \text{selling price per unit)}}$$

H. The C-V-P model can be used to determine selling prices to earn a target profit given a specified volume, calculate a new breakeven point if either fixed or variable costs (or both) were to change, and assist in sensitivity analysis (what-if assumptions).

I. Another calculation derived from C-V-P analysis is the **margin of safety**. The margin of safety is the excess of the projected (or actual) sales over the breakeven sales level. It is a measure of how much a forecast can be incorrect and the company still be profitable.

J. Graphically, the relationships between costs, volume, and profit can be depicted using all the variables, or can be condensed to show only the profit in relation to volume. The later presentation utilizes the contribution margin concept.

K. In multiproduct firms, it is more useful to perform breakeven analysis using **the contribution margin ratio**. The contribution margin ratio is the contribution margin as a percentage of sales. Thus, the breakeven formula can also be expressed as:

$$\text{Breakeven Sales Dollars} = \frac{\text{Fixed Costs}}{\text{Contribution Margin Ratio}}$$

L. The effect of income taxes can be incorporated in the model by substituting after-tax profits for before-tax profits using this relationship:

$$\text{After-tax Profit} = \text{Before-tax Profit} \times (1 - \text{Tax Rate})$$

M. The **contribution format** for income reporting is more conducive for C-V-P analysis than the traditional format. The contribution format helps managers focus on variable costs on a unit basis and fixed costs on a lump-sum basis. The manager's short-run objective is to maximize a product's contribution margin because it is assumed that fixed costs will not change.

N. If a firm uses full absorption costing for external purposes, the reported profit will be the same as that reported using the contribution format only when there is no change in inventory. If changes in inventory occur, the two approaches can be reconciled by using the same techniques used in comparing variable costing with absorption costing.

O. Multiproduct firms performing C-V-P analysis must make one of four assumptions in order to determine a breakeven point, namely (1) **assume the same contribution margin for all products**, (2) **assume a fixed product mix**, (3) **assume a weighted-average contribution margin** or (4) **treat each product line as a separate entity**.

P. The C-V-P model has four underlying assumptions: (1) **Total costs are partitioned into fixed and variable components**; (2) **Cost and revenue behavior is linear throughout the relevant range of activity**; (3) **Product mix remains constant throughout the relevant range of activity**; and (4) **There is no change in inventory**.

SELF-TEST AND PRACTICE EXERCISES

A. **MATCHING**

Match each of the following terms with its meaning.

Term	Meaning
___1. Relevant range	a. The excess of projected sales over breakeven sales level.
___2. Contribution margin ratio	b. The point where the company earns zero profit.
___3. Cost-volume-profit	c. The volumes at which the cost relationships are valid.
___4. P-V graph	d. Sales less cost of goods sold.
___5. Margin of safety	e. Enables managers to respond to "what-if" questions.
___6. Breakeven point	f. Selling price less variable costs per unit.
___7. Gross margin	g. Relationship between costs and profits at different volumes.
___8. Sensitivity analysis	h. Contribution margin as a percentage of the selling price.
___9. Contribution margin per unit	i. The relationship between profit and volume.

B. GRAPHING COST RELATIONSHIPS

   REQUIRED:

   1. Label the points, lines or areas on the following cost-volume-profit graph:

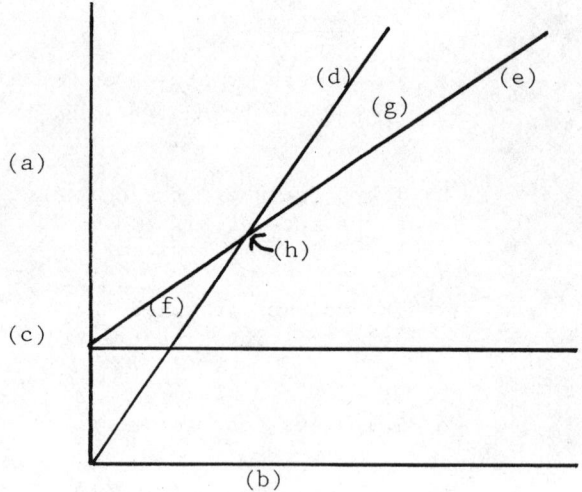

(a) _____   (e) _____

(b) _____   (f) _____

(c) _____   (g) _____

(d) _____   (h) _____

2. Label the points, lines or areas on the following profit-volume graph:

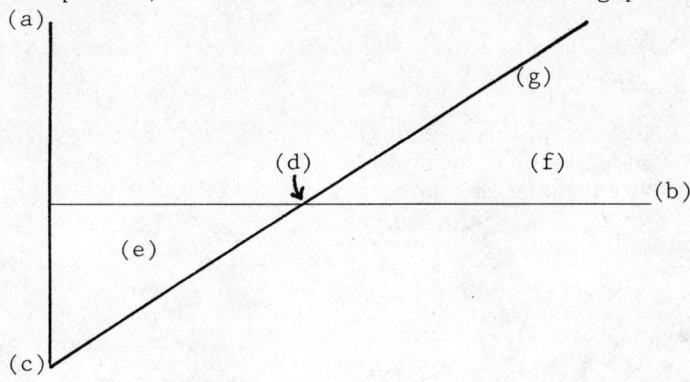

(a) _____   (d) _____

(b) _____   (e) _____

(c) _____   (f) _____

                                            (g) _____

C. **COST-VOLUME PROFIT ANALYSIS**

Given for the Laing Company:

Selling price per unit	$9.00
Variable cost per unit	$6.30
Fixed costs per period	$27,000.00

REQUIRED:

1. Breakeven point in units. _____

2. Breakeven point in sales. $_____

3. Sales that would produce a profit of $9,000. $_____

4. Units needed to breakeven if variable costs increased to $7.00. _____

5. Volume needed to earn a 10% return on sales. Show a proof of this calculation. _____

6. Selling price to earn a target profit of $10,000 assuming the company expects to sell 12,000 units. $_____

D. CHOOSING BETWEEN TWO ALTERNATIVES

A manager is trying to choose between two alternative product lines, A & B. The following information is available:

	A	B
Selling price	$8	$8
Variable costs	$5	$6
Fixed costs	$300	$200
Estimated volume	125 units	150 units

REQUIRED:

1. Calculate the breakeven point for product A. _____

2. Calculate the breakeven point for product B. _____

3. What is the margin of safety for product A? _____

4. What is the margin of safety for product B? _____

5. What is the expected profit for product A? _____

6. What is the expected profit for product B? _____

7. Which product should the manager accept? Why? _____
_____

E. A MULTIPRODUCT COMPANY AND BREAKEVEN ANALYSIS

A company sells three products, X, Y and Z. The company has fixed costs in the amount of $2400. The following information is presented to you:

	X	Y	Z
Price per unit	$10	$5	$7
Variable costs per unit	$6	$2	$6
Number of units sold	1,000	2,000	2,000

REQUIRED:

Assuming the product mix will be the same at the breakeven point, compute the breakeven in:

1. total units_____

2. units by product line _____

3. sales dollars at breakeven point by product line (Prepare a contribution format income statement to prove these sales will result in a breakeven position for the company)

_____
_____
_____
_____
_____
_____

4. Why wouldn't the company breakeven if it sold the 1,000 units of product Z only?

_____
_____

SOLUTIONS

A. MATCHING:

   1. c   2. h   3. g   4. i

   5. a   6. b   7. d   8. e   9. f

B. GRAPHING COST RELATIONSHIPS:

   1. a. dollars   e. total costs
      b. volume   f. loss area
      c. fixed costs   g. profit area
      d. total revenue   h. breakeven point

   2. a. dollars   d. breakeven point
      b. volume   e. loss area
      c. fixed costs   f. profit area
                                g. contribution margin

C. COST-VOLUME-PROFIT ANALYSIS:

   1. Breakeven in units $= \dfrac{\text{Fixed costs}}{\text{Contribution margin}} = \dfrac{\$27{,}000}{\$9 - \$6.30}$

                                                                 $= \dfrac{\$27{,}000}{\$2.70}$

                                                                   $= 10{,}000$ units

   2. Breakeven in sales dollars $= \dfrac{\text{Fixed costs}}{\text{Contribution margin ratio}}$

     where the Contribution margin ratio $= \dfrac{\text{Contribution margin}}{\text{Sales}}$

     therefore, Breakeven in sales $= \dfrac{\$27{,}000}{\$2.70/\$9.00} = \dfrac{\$27{,}000}{.3} = \$90{,}000$

3. Sales to earn a target profit = $\dfrac{\text{Fixed costs + Target profit}}{\text{Contribution margin ratio}}$

$$= \dfrac{\$27,000 + \$9,000}{.3} = \dfrac{\$36,000}{.3}$$

$$= \$120,000$$

Another way to solve this would be the incremental approach. That is, how many dollars over breakeven does the company need to cover the desired profit of $9,000. Since the contribution margin ratio is .3, then $9,000/.3 = $30,000 additional sales beyond the breakeven point of $90,000, or a total of $120,000.

4. New breakeven = $\dfrac{\text{Fixed costs}}{\text{New contribution margin}} = \dfrac{\$27,000}{\$9 - \$7} = 13,500$ units

5. Since target profit is a percentage of sales, treat it as a variable cost.

Target profit = $\dfrac{\text{Fixed cost}}{\text{Contribution margin} - .1 \text{ (selling price)}}$

$$= \dfrac{\$27,000}{\$2.70 - .1(\$9)} = \dfrac{\$27,000}{\$1.80} = 15,000 \text{ units}$$

Proof:
Sales (15,000 units @ $9)	$135,000
Variable cost (15,000 units @ $6.30)	94,500
Contribution margin	$ 40,500
Less: Fixed cost	27,000
Operating profit (10% of sales)	$ 13,500

6. Total revenue = variable cost + fixed cost + profit

(Units)(selling price) = units(variable cost) + fixed cost + profit

12,000 (X) = 12,000 ($6.30) + 27,000 + 10,000

12,000 (X) = 75,600 + 27,000 + 10,000

12,000 (X) = 112,600

(X) = 112,600/12,000 or $9.38

D. CHOOSING BETWEEN TWO ALTERNATIVES:

1. $\dfrac{\text{Fixed cost}}{\text{Contribution margin}} = \dfrac{300}{8-5} = \dfrac{300}{3} = 100 \text{ units}$

2. $\dfrac{\text{Fixed cost}}{\text{Contribution margin}} = \dfrac{200}{8-6} = \dfrac{200}{2} = 100 \text{ units}$

3. $\dfrac{\text{Sales - Breakeven sales}}{\text{Sales}} = \dfrac{125 - 100}{125} = \dfrac{25}{125} = 20\%$

4. $\dfrac{\text{Sales - Breakeven sales}}{\text{Sales}} = \dfrac{150 - 100}{150} = \dfrac{50}{150} = 33\ 1/3\%$

5. Sales 125 units @ 8 $1,000
    Variable cost 125 units @ 5   625

    Contribution margin $ 375
    Fixed cost   300
    Operating profit $ 75

6. Sales 150 units @ 8 $1,200
    Variable cost 150 units @ 6   900

    Contribution margin $ 300
    Fixed cost   200
    Operating profit $ 100

7. The manager should chose product B. It has the higher margin of safety and higher expected profit even though it has the lower contribution margin per unit.

E. A MULTIPRODUCT COMPANY AND BREAKEVEN ANALYSIS:

1. First compute the weighted-average contribution margin:

		X	Y	Z
a.	Contribution margin	4	3	1
b.	Product mix	100/500	200/500	200/500
c.	Product mix stated as a decimal	.2	.4	.4
d.	(a) times (c)	.8	1.2	.4
e.	Weighted average (sum of line d)				2.4

83

Next, substitute in breakeven formula:

$$\text{Breakeven} = \frac{\text{Fixed costs}}{\text{Weighted-average contribution margin}}$$

$$= \frac{2,400}{2.4} = 1,000 \text{ units}$$

2. Number of X units = .2 (1,000) = 200 units
   Number of Y units = .4 (1,000) = 400 units
   Number of Z units = .4 (1,000) = 400 units

3.

	X	Y	Z	Total
Sales	2,000	2,000	2,800	6,800
Variable costs	1,200	800	2,400	4,400
Contribution margin	800	1,200	400	2,400
Fixed cost				2,400
Operating profit				0

4. If 1,000 units of Z were sold, the total contribution margin would only be $1,000 [($7-$6)(1,000 units)]. The company must sell higher margin units in order to breakeven.

STUDY PLAN

1. Review the graphs in Exhibits 7.1 and Exhibit 7.2. Be sure you understand that the same information can be presented using these two different formats. The profit-volume graph is more useful in communicating with managers who focus on volume rather than costs, such as marketing managers.

2. Review all four self-study problems.

3. Derive the breakeven formula yourself. Begin with the equation format, Profit = Total Revenues - Total Costs. Then substitute zero for Profit. Next, divide total costs into its fixed and variable components. Then show revenue and variable costs as a function of units sold. Finally, define the difference between the selling price and the variable costs per unit as the contribution margin. Your result should be the breakeven formula, x = fixed costs/contribution margin per unit.

Do Exercise 18 using the algebraic equation first, then the breakeven formula. You should find the formula approach quicker to use.

4. Review the following outline.

REVIEW OUTLINE

I. Cost-volume-profit decisions.

   A. Short-run orientation. (Assumes fixed costs unchanged)

   B. Cost-volume-profit equation.

   1. Profit = revenues - costs

   2. Profit = revenues - variable costs - fixed costs

   3. Profit = total contribution margin - fixed costs

   C. Breakeven point.

   1. The breakeven point is the volume where total revenue equals total costs.

   2. The breakeven point in units is determined by dividing fixed costs by the contribution margin per unit.

   3. The breakeven point in sales dollars is determined by dividing fixed costs by the contribution margin ratio.

   D. The cost-volume-profit graph depicts the relationship of costs, volume, and profit and identifies the breakeven point. An alternative graph is called the profit-volume graph.

   E. The contribution margin per unit is the excess of the unit's selling price over the unit's variable cost. The contribution margin can also refer to the total selling price less all variable costs.

   F. Application of the cost-volume-profit model. In general, the cost-volume-profit model can be used when certain parts of the model are known but one part is unknown.

   1. For example, selling price can be determined if volume, fixed costs, and variable costs are known.

2. Or, if we know all variables, we can determine the target volume necessary to earn either a fixed profit or a specified rate of return on sales.

G. The margin of safety is the excess of projected (or actual) sales over the breakeven sales level.

H. Limitations of the cost-volume-profit model.

1. The variable and fixed cost estimates in the model may not be valid, particularly if the analysis is for volume outside of the relevant range used to make the estimates.

2. The simple model may not be useful for multiproduct firms.

3. The model considers only those factors that can be quantified.

I. Underlying assumptions about the cost-volume-profit model.

1. Total cost can be broken down into fixed and variable components.

2. Determination of the breakeven point requires:

a. Selling price per unit, total fixed cost, and variable cost per unit will not change as the activity level changes.

b. Production mix and sales mix are constant.

II. Contribution Reporting.

A. Managers should prefer the contribution format for internal reporting.

1. It helps them focus on unit variable costs.

2. It assists in evaluating the short-run profitability of products.

B. Income reported under the contribution approach will differ from external reports using GAAP except in the following situations:

1. There is no change in inventory.

2. Revenues are equal to cash inflows, and costs, other than depreciation, are equal to cash outflows.

CHAPTER 8

SHORT-RUN DECISIONS AND DIFFERENTIAL ANALYSIS

Managers make short-run decisions such as pricing and accepting special orders. This chapter introduces the concept of differential analysis which provides a framework for managers to make financially sound decisions. Other decisions which normally involve long-range projections can also be made using differential analysis if no additional capacity is required. Examples of these decisions are make-or-buy and dropping product lines.

CHAPTER HIGHLIGHTS

A. Management decision-making is the process of making choices. **Differential analysis** (also known as incremental or marginal analysis) is the analysis of differences among particular alternative actions.

B. The differential model is an extension of the cost-volume-profit model. However, instead of giving all the elements equal attention, only the differences between alternatives are highlighted. By using the differential approach, managers make more efficient use of their time, especially in complex problems where there are many variables and only a few change.

C. In differential analysis, only those elements which change are considered **relevant**. While fixed costs are nearly always differential in long-run decisions involving capacity changes, they are only sometimes differential in short-run operating decisions.

D. Differential analysis emphasizes cash flows. While the timing of cash flows is very important, students must first deal with differences in the amount of cash flow.

E. Cash flow is a useful measure for differential analysis, but, it overlooks two costs: **opportunity cost** and **economic depreciation**.

F. **Economic depreciation** is the change in the economic value of an asset during its use. When focusing on cash flows, economic depreciation is captured by the difference between the cash paid to acquire an asset at the original purchase date and the salvage or trade-in value received for the asset when it is sold. Managers must consider the sales value, if any, on the date of disposal because it is a relevant cost.

G. Decisions regarding the prices to be charged for a firm's products are complex. In a competitive environment, companies often must accept the going market price. However, firms with cost plus fixed fee contracts have some control over prices charged. Managers must understand the relevant costs of a product in order to make sound pricing decisions.

H. If a firm is to remain in business in the long run, it must recover all of its costs and provide for an adequate return to its owners. In cost-based pricing, managers must determine which costs will be covered. In addition, they must understand the concept of decreasing fixed cost per unit as a result of increasing volume. In general, full cost-based pricing can lead to incorrect decisions because it ignores differential analysis.

I. The differential approach to pricing presumes that the price must be at least equal to the differential cost of the product. Of course, managers may decide to sell a product below its cost for a particular marketing strategy. For most goods, a sale should at least cover the fixed and variable costs associated with the product, and preferably should contribute to fixed costs and then to the profits of the company. The product's differential cost sets a minimum selling price for the unit. The differential approach leads to correct short-run pricing as long as the company obtains the highest possible price for the unit over its differential costs.

J. Other decisions that often involve long-range strategies but could be evaluated using differential analysis include make-or-buy decisions and adding or dropping product lines.

K. A decision in which a firm decides to meet its needs, either internally or externally, is a **make-or-buy** decision. This analysis is made difficult as a result of the numerous hard to quantify variables such as quality, dependability and the probability of outsider vendors raising their prices in the future. While usually this decision is made considering the long-run implications for the company, the impact of the decision on current profits can be calculated using differential analysis.

L. Managers must decide when to add or drop products from the product line and when to open or abandon sales territories. While this is another example of a decision that has tremendous long-run implications for the company, the impact of this decision on current profits can also be determined using differential analysis.

M. The **differential principle** dictates that when differential revenues exceed differential costs, the manager should accept the proposal. This conclusion assumes there is no other better alternative available.

N. Allocating common fixed expenses often provides misleading information to managers because the company must absorb common fixed costs even if the order is not sold or if the product is not dropped.

O. Inventory management can also be understood in terms of differential analysis. For inventory, there are two kinds of costs: ordering (set-up) and carrying costs. The total inventory cost is the sum of the carrying and ordering costs.

P. **Carrying costs** include storage costs, insurance, losses due to inventory damage and theft, property taxes and the opportunity cost of funds tied up in inventory.

Q. The **economic order quantity** (EOQ) is the optimal number of units ordered or produced. The EOQ can be calculated by a formula or by trial and error. Managers should use differential analysis to understand the impact of alternative inventory levels on profits.

R. **Safety stocks** are buffers against running out of inventory. The EOQ formula does not determine the amount of safety stock. Managers select a level based on competition, cost of idle productive facilities and loss of customer goodwill.

S. **Just-in-time** (JIT) inventory is a method of managing inventories and the demand for inventories that reduces inventory levels virtually to zero. Each item in production is made immediately as needed in the next step in the production process.

SELF-TEST AND PRACTICE EXERCISES

A. **MATCHING**

Match each of the following terms with its meaning.

<u>Term</u>

___ 1. Economic depreciation

___ 2. Set-up costs

___ 3. Make-or-buy decision

___ 4. Differential analysis

___ 5. Carrying costs

___ 6. Opportunity costs

___ 7. Safety stock

___ 8. Cost-based pricing

___ 9. Economic order quantity

___ 10. Just-in-time

<u>Meaning</u>

a. Optimal number of items in a production run or order.

b. The cost of holding or storing inventory from the time of purchase until the time of sale.

c. The analysis of differences among alternatives.

d. The benefits from alternative use of assets.

e. The decrease or increase in the value of an asset during its use.

f. Buffer stock that is held to avoid stockouts.

g. Adding a markup to the firm's costs.

h. Any decision in which a firm decides whether to meet its needs internally or to acquire goods and services outside the firm.

i. The cost of preparing machinery for each productive run.

j. An inventory management technique where inventory is produced only as needed in the next production run.

B. SPECIAL ORDER

The Exer Company has the capacity to produce 8,000 units per year. It's predicted operations for the year are:

Sales	6,000 units @ $10 each	$60,000

Manufacturing costs:

Variable	$4 per unit
Fixed	$15,000

Marketing & Administrative

Variable	$1 per unit
Fixed	$4,000

REQUIRED:

1. Prepare an projected income statement for the coming year:

_____
_____
_____
_____
_____
_____
_____
_____

2. Should the company accept a special order for 1,000 units at a selling price of $8? There are no variable marketing and administrative costs for this order and regular sales will not be affected. What is the impact of this decision on profits?

_____
_____

3. Suppose there was a one-time set up fee of $1,000 for the order in part 2. Should the special order be accepted? Why?

_____

_____

4. Should the original manufacturing fixed costs be allocated to the special order before making the decision?

_____

_____

C. **MAKE OR BUY DECISION**

Segar Company, a radio manufacturer, is currently producing 5,000 radios a year. It manufactures its own parts and cases. Then it assembles the product. The following are the current costs of the department that manufactures the parts:

Material	$3
Labor	4
Factory overhead, direct	5
Factory overhead, allocated	2
Cost per unit	$14

Another company offered to supply Segar with all the parts it needs at a cost of $13.

REQUIRED:

1. Should Segar buy the part from outside the company? Assume the facilities would be idle.

_____

_____

2. If Segar could rent the parts department space for $9,000 should it rent the space and buy the parts it needs from the outside vendor?

_____

_____

3. One manager at Segar noted that the factory overhead absorbed by the parts department is $25,000 ($5/unit @ 5,000 units). The manager wants to know how this factor was considered in your analysis.

___

___

___

D. DROPPING A PRODUCT LINE

Given for the Essbey Company:

	Ice Cream	Candy	Cards	Total
Sales	$20	$15	$10	$45
Variable costs	10	10	8	28
Contribution Margin	10	5	2	17
Fixed costs (allocated equally to departments)	5	5	5	15
Operating profit	5	0	(3)	2

REQUIRED:

1. If no other alternative exists for the cards department, should the company drop the cards product line? Prepare an income statement showing what would happen to profits if cards were dropped.

___

___

___

___

___

___

2. Prepare an income statement by product line if Candy was dropped and the common fixed costs were allocated equally to the remaining departments.

3. Referring to question 2, why did the Candy department go from a "breakeven" position to a loss position? Should it be dropped?

4. What if the common fixed costs were originally allocated $10 to ice cream, $4 to candy and $1 to cards. Would you change any of your decisions? Prepare a revised income statement.

E. ECONOMIC ORDER QUANTITY

(Use trial and error or the model in Appendix B)

The Fancy Free Company regularly uses 10 units per day, 300 days per year. Units cost $2 each. Ordering costs are $10 per order and the holding costs of items in inventory are estimated to be 10% of cost per year.

REQUIRED:

1. Complete the following table:

a. units	100	200	300	500	1000	3000
b. number of orders	____	____	____	____	____	____
c. ordering costs	____	____	____	____	____	____
d. average inventory	____	____	____	____	____	____
e. average cost in inventory	____	____	____	____	____	____
f. carrying costs	____	____	____	____	____	____
g. ordering costs + carrying costs	____	____	____	____	____	____

2. Compute (or estimate) the economic order quantity.

3. How many orders will the company place? _____

SOLUTIONS

A. MATCHING:

    1. e 2. i 3. h 4. c 5. b

    6. d 7. f 8. g 9. a 10. j

B. SPECIAL ORDER:

1.
Sales		$60,000
Less variable cost of goods sold:		
Manufacturing	$24,000	
Marketing	6,000	30,000
Contribution margin		30,000
Less fixed costs		
Manufacturing	$15,000	
Marketing	4,000	19,000
Operating profit		$11,000

2. Yes. The contribution margin on this order is $4 ($8 - $4). Thus, the 1000 units would contribute $4,000 (1,000 units @ $4) to the profits of the company. Profits would increase to $15,000.

3. Yes. The incremental contribution margin of $4,000 less the incremental fixed costs of $1,000 would generate $3,000 additional operating profit for the company.

4. No. Only the differential costs should be considered in analyzing the special order.

C. MAKE OR BUY DECISION:

1. No. The incremental costs of Materials ($3), labor ($4) and factory overhead ($5), or $12, are less than the suggested $13 price of the part if acquired from the outside vendor. If the company accepts the offer, this year's profits will decrease by $5,000 ($1 per unit @ 5000 units).

2. Yes. The loss of $5,000 will be more than offset by the $9,000 additional revenue. The company's profits will increase by $4,000.

3. Fixed costs were not relevant because they would not change in the short run. Therefore, they were not considered.

D. DROPPING A PRODUCT LINE:

1.
Sales ($20 + $15)	$ 35
Less variable costs ($10 + $10)	20
Contribution margin	$15
Less fixed costs	15
Operating profits	$ 0

Profit declined by $2 because the company no longer benefitted from the contribution of the cards department.

2.
	Ice Cream	Candy
Sales	$20.00	$15.00
Less variable costs	10.00	10.00
Contribution margin	$10.00	$ 5.00
Less fixed costs	7.50	7.50
Operating profits	$ 2.50	$(2.50)

3. No. Candy contributed $5 to the recovery of fixed costs. The change in profits is due solely to the allocation method and not to any differential cost.

4.
	Ice Cream	Candy	Cards	Total
Sales	$20	$15	$10	$45
Less variable costs	10	10	8	28
Contribution margin	$10	$ 5	$ 2	$17
Less fixed costs	10	4	1	15
Operating profits	$ 0	$ 1	$ 1	$ 2

No decision would change. The allocation method only affects how the overall profit of $2 is divided among the departments.

E. ECONOMIC ORDER QUANTITY:

1.

a. units	100	200	300	500	1000	3000
b. number of orders	30	15	10	6	3	1
c. ordering costs	$300	150	100	60	30	10
d. average inventory	50	100	150	250	500	1500
e. average cost in inventory	$100	200	300	500	1000	3000
f. carrying costs	10	20	30	50	100	300
g. ordering costs + carrying costs	$310	170	130	110	130	310

2. About 500 units. Using the formula, the EOQ is approximately 548 units.

3. There will be 6 orders.

STUDY PLAN

1. The concept of differential analysis assists managers in making short-run decisions. Review Exhibit 8.4 in the text to be sure you understand that differential costs set a minimum price to be charged. In the long run, companies must not only meet their fixed costs but also generate a return to the owners.

2. Study the section on incorrect use of accounting data which begins on page 308. It is important to remember that accounting data intended for inventory costing for external financial reports is not necessarily the best information for managerial decision making.

3. Review Problem 2 for self-study. Note the status quo is used as the reference point for comparing all alternatives. Using differential analysis, the impact of numerous alternatives can be considered efficiently.

4. Review the following outline.

CHAPTER OUTLINE

I. The differential principle.

    A. Managerial decision making is the process of making choices. Differences between choices is highlighted by differential analysis.

    B. Financial decisions are made considering the amount and timing of cash flows. Differential analysis only considers the differences in amount of cash flow.

    C. Many decisions require projections into the future, but the impact on operating profits for the current year can be determined using differential analysis.

II. Pricing decisions.

    A. In some cases, firms are in competitive markets and have little control over prices; however, in many situations, firms do have some control over prices, and they may use cost information to help set prices.

    B. Cost-based approach to pricing.

        1. In the long run, a firm must recover all of its costs plus provide an adequate return on the capital provided by owners.

        2. If the full-cost approach to pricing is used, companies might not always make the best decision for the firm because:

            a. Costs attributable to a particular product are affected by such questionable practices as the failure to recognize the opportunity cost and economic depreciation associated with the asset, and the allocation of costs to specific products on an arbitrary basis.

            b. There is a circularity in pricing decisions when the cost-based approach is used because price, volume and cost are all interrelated.

    C. The incremental approach to pricing.

        1. The incremental approach to pricing is based on the premise that the price must at least equal the incremental cost of producing and selling the product. In the short run, these might be only the variable costs of production.

        2. Incremental pricing is particularly useful for special orders and for sales when the plant is operating below capacity.

III. Other decisions.

    A. Inventory management decisions can be analyzed by differential analysis.

        1. The optimal number of units to produce or order is determined by comparing costs at various amounts and selecting the point at which total costs are minimal.

        2. The costs associated with inventory are ordering costs and carrying costs.

        3. Just-in-time inventory systems reduce inventories to virtually zero. Each item is produced only when it is needed for the next step in the production process.

    B. Choosing the optimal product mix when there are capacity limitations requires not only estimating the differential cost per unit, but also the differential cost per unit of scarce resource consumed by the product.

CHAPTER 9

LONG-RUN DECISIONS AND CAPITAL BUDGETING

In this chapter we shift our attention to long-run decisions. We focus on decisions to change plant or operating capacity. These decisions are analyzed in terms of differences in cash flows and in the timing of cash flows. When cash flows extend over several future periods with different patterns for various alternatives, we use present value analysis to make cash flows comparable.

CHAPTER HIGHLIGHTS

A. Short-run operating decisions and long-run capacity decisions are similar because they both rely on incremental analysis of cash inflows and outflows. Long-run capacity decisions, however, must also consider the timing of cash flows that take place over several future periods.

B. **Discounted cash flows** (DCF) methods are designed to aid in the evaluation of investments involving cash flows over time. The underlying premise is that a dollar received today is worth more than a dollar received in the future because today's dollar can be invested and earn at least a risk-free return (interest).

C. **Capital budgeting** refers to making decisions about which long-term investments should be selected and how they should be financed. The capital budget decision involves estimating future cash flows, deciding on an appropriate interest rate for discounting those cash flows, and, if accepted, deciding how to finance the project.

D. **Discounted cash flow methods** are designed to aid the evaluation of investments involving cash flows over time, where the time elapsed between the cash payment and the receipts is significant. Two common discounted cash flow methods are the net present value and the internal rate of return.

E. The **net present value** (NPV) method involves: (1) estimating future cash inflows and cash outflows for each alternative, (2) discounting the future cash flows to the present, using the firm's cost of capital, and (3) accepting the proposed project or selections from a set of mutually exclusive projects. If the NPV for an alternative is positive, it should be accepted.

F. The cash flows associated with an investment project include the initial cash flows, the periodic cash flows, and the terminal cash flows.

G. **Initial cash outflows** include the original asset cost, freight, installation, and any income tax payments on disposal of existing assets at a gain. Initial cash inflows include the salvage value of the existing asset, tax credits on the new asset, and the reduction of income tax if the existing asset is sold at a loss. Initial cash inflows and outflows are not discounted because they already reflect equivalent current dollars paid or received as a result of the transaction.

H. **Periodic cash flows** include revenue and expenses that occur throughout the life of the project. Periodic cash flows must be discounted by the appropriate discount rates in order to determine the equivalent amount in current dollars that would be received or paid out.

I. **Terminal cash flows** include the proceeds from disposing of the new asset and any additional tax if the asset is sold at a gain (or the reduction in taxes if the asset is sold at a loss). Terminal cash flows are restated in terms of current dollars by using a single discount rate.

J. When the cash flows are restated in terms of current values, and then summed, a positive present value indicates the project will generate at least the desired return. A negative value indicates the project will not generate the necessary return. A zero present value indicates the project's expected return is exactly equal to the rate of return used in the analysis.

K. Since income taxes affect both the amount and timing of cash flows, they must be considered in making investment decisions. Similarly, since depreciation methods and alternative investment credit benefits affect income taxes paid, investment decisions must be analyzed using all possible combinations allowed.

L. The appropriate discount rate is the firm's cost of capital. The term **cost of capital** means the minimum rate of return required by the owner of an asset to justify using it. Because the firm could invest its resources in alternative projects that earn at least the cost of its capital, the cost of capital is considered the firm's opportunity cost.

M. The cost of capital used in making investments should focus on the assets. The cost of funds needed to finance the asset is an independent decision that is made after the feasibility of the project is determined. The acquisition or financing of the asset is a separate decision from the investment decision.

N. Since the net present value method requires three types of estimates, namely, the amount and timing of cash flows and the cost of capital rate, sensitivity analysis can be used to see what would happen if these estimates changed.

O. There are numerous complications in trying to estimate future cash flows in real situations. In order to avoid unnecessary confusion in complex situations, it is better to construct a series of mutually exclusive investment alternatives in order to evaluate each, and choose the best.

P. No special treatment is needed for working capital. The focus of capital budgeting is on the amount and timing of cash flows. Thus, the technique adequately captures working capital changes in the company.

Q. Inflation is considered in arriving at the cost of capital rate. However, decision makers must also include in their analysis the effects of anticipated inflation on the cash flows.

SELF-TEST AND PRACTICE EXERCISES

USE THE FOLLOWING DISCOUNT FACTORS FOR SOLVING THE EXERCISES:

DISCOUNT FACTORS FOR 10%

PERIOD	PRESENT VALUE OF $1.00	PRESENT VALUE OF $1.00 PER PERIOD RECEIVED AT END OF PERIOD
1	.91	.91
2	.83	1.74
3	.75	2.49
4	.68	3.17
5	.62	3.79

A. MATCHING

Match each of the following terms with its meaning.

    Term

___1. Net present value of cash flows

___2. Opportunity cost of capital to stockholders

___3. Mutually exclusive projects

___4. Capital budgeting

___5. Initial cash flows

___6. Terminal cash flows

___7. Periodic cash flows

___8. Average cost of capital for the firm

    Meaning

a. The average rate that must be paid for funds invested.

b. Cash flows occurring during the life of the project.

c. Discounted value of all cash inflows and outflows of a project at a given discount rate.

d. Competing investment projects where accepting one project eliminates the possibility of taking the remaining projects.

e. The process of choosing investment projects by considering the present value of cash flows and deciding how to raise funds required.

f. Cash flow associated with investment projects at inception.

g. The opportunity cost of placing capital in one investment and foregoing the return from alternative investments.

h. Cash flows occurring at the conclusion of the project.

B. COMPUTE THE NET PRESENT VALUE

A firm has an after-tax cost of capital of 10%. It is considering investing in the following projects:

	Project A	Project B
Initial cost	$4,000	$4,000
Periodic cash flows (Received at year-end)		
Year 1	2,000	2,000
Year 2	2,000	1,000
Year 3	2,000	3,000
Total	6,000	6,000

REQUIRED:

1. Calculate the net present value of project A. Use the table found at the beginning of the practice exercises.

2. Calculate the net present value of project B. Use the table found at the beginning of the practice exercises.

___

3. Both projects cost $4,000 and generate $6,000 of cash flows over the life of the asset. Why are the net present values different?

___

C. DIFFERENT DISCOUNT RATES

An investment of $3,000 today will yield $1,000 a year at the end of each of the next four years.

REQUIRED: (Use the tables found in the back of the text).

1. Will the investment be accepted if the cost of capital is 10%? _____

2. Will the investment be accepted if the cost of capital is 12%? _____

3. Will the investment be accepted if the cost of capital is 20%? _____

D. DISPOSAL OF A CURRENTLY OWNED ASSET

You are given the following present value factors at 8%, the Yontz Company's minimum desired rate of return.

End of Period	Present Value of $1	Present Value of an Annuity of $1
1	0.93	0.93
2	0.86	1.78
3	0.79	2.58
4	0.74	3.31
5	0.68	3.99
6	0.63	4.62

The Yontz Company is considering the replacement of a piece of equipment. The old machine has a book value of $800 and a remaining estimated life of 5 years with no salvage value at that time. Present salvage value is $200. The new equipment will cost $1,200, including transportation and installation. It has an estimated life of 5 years with no salvage value. Annual cash operating costs are $500 for the old machine and $150 for the new machine.

REQUIRED:

1. What is the present value of the operating cash outflows for the old machine?

2. What is the present value of the operating cash outflows for the new machine?

3. What is the present value of all incremental benefits and operating savings if the new machine is purchased?

4. What is the differential or incremental investment that is required?

5. Using a differential approach, what is the net present value of the replacement alternative?

SOLUTIONS

A. MATCHING:

    1. c   2. g   3. d   4. e

    5. f   6. h   7. b   8. a

B. COMPUTE THE NET PRESENT VALUE:

    1. Project A

	Amount	Discount factor	Present Value
a. Initial outlay	(4,000)	1.00	$(4,000)
b. Cash inflows (see below)			
Year 1	2,000	.91	1,820
Year 2	2,000	.83	1,660
Year 3	2,000	.75	1,500
c. Net present value			$ 980

    Alternative calculation of cash inflows:

        2,000 for 3 years @ 10% = 2,000 (2.49) = 4,980

    2. Project B

	Amount	Discount factor	Present Value
a. Initial outlay	(4,000)	1.00	$(4,000)
b. Cash inflows			
Year 1	2,000	.91	1,820
Year 2	1,000	.83	830
Year 3	3,000	.75	2,250
c. Net present value			$ 900

    3. The time value of money explains the difference. The project that generates $1,000 more cash in year 2 is worth more to the company because the company can take the cash and invest it in other projects.

C. DIFFERENT DISCOUNT RATES:

    1. Yes, the present value is +170. (-3,000 + 3,170)

    2. Yes, the present value is + 37. (-3,000 + 3,037)

    3. No, the present value is -411. (-3,000 + 2,589)

D. DISPOSAL OF A CURRENTLY OWNED ASSET:

1. PV = $500 x 3.99
     = $1,995

2. PV = $150 x 3.99
     = $598.50

3. Incremental cash savings = $350
   Salvage value   = $200
   Present value   = $200 + ($350 x 3.99)
                            = $200 + $1,396.50
                            = $1,596.50

4. $1,200 - $200 = $1,000

5. $1,596.50 - $1,000 = $596.50

STUDY PLAN

1. Redo Self-study problem 1 in the text assuming that the cost of capital is changed to 15%. (Now is a good time to learn how to use a computer-assisted spreadsheet software program like Joe or Lotus 1-2-3.) Would the company accept the project under these new assumptions? The solution is given below.

Cash flow from investment:

	Amount	Discount Factor	Present Value
Year 1	12,600	.870	10,962
2	17,520	.756	13,245
3	16,068	.658	10,573
4	15,420	.572	8,820
5	16,200	.497	8,051
6	15,192	.432	6,563

Operating cash flows   58,214
Cash outlay for machinery   (60,000)
Salvage value from selling machine
   $6,000 x .432   2,592
Taxes on gain of $6,000
   $6,000 x .40 x .432   (1,037)
Net Present Value   (237)

Since the net present value is negative, the company would not accept this investment.

2. Review the chapter outline.

CHAPTER OUTLINE

I. Long-run decisions.

   A. Similar to short-run decisions because both rely on differential principle.

   B. Involves cash flows over many periods.

   C. Some technique must be employed for making cash flows from different time periods comparable.

II. Capital budgeting.

   A. Involves decisions about which long-term investments to undertake and how to finance them.

   B. Investment decisions should be made independently of finance decisions.

   C. Capital budgeting requires estimating future cash flows, deciding on a discount rate and discounting the cash flows to the same, usually present, time.

III. Discounted cash flow methods.

   A. The net present value method involves the following steps:

      1. Estimating the amounts of future cash inflows and future cash outflows for each alternative under consideration.

      2. Discounting the future cash flow to the present by using the cost of capital, which considers the risk of the alternative.

      3. Accepting or rejecting the proposed project based on the following decision rule: If the net present value of the future cash flows is positive, the alternative should be accepted; if the net present value is negative, the alternative should be rejected.

B. The cost of capital. The appropriate discount rate to use in evaluating investment projects is the opportunity cost of foregoing similar alternatives.

C. There is likely to be some error in each of the predictions or estimates employed in the analysis. Sensitivity analysis allows the analyst to determine the impact of various assumptions about the three variables used: the amount and timing of cash flows as well as the cost of capital used.

IV. Complications in computing periodic cash flows.

   A. New asset acquisition: deriving the net proceeds when assets are retired.

   B. Disposal of currently owned assets: sale or trade-in.

   C. Depreciation and its impact on cash flow.

   D. Salvage value of disposed assets.

   E. Impact of working capital.

V. Effects of inflation on the cost of capital and cash flows.

   A. Cost of capital includes:

      1. A "pure" or real rate of interest.

      2. A risk factor.

      3. A premium reflecting expected inflation.

   B. Cost of capital reflects general inflation.

CHAPTER 10

CAPITAL BUDGETING: A CLOSER LOOK

Capital budgeting is a very complex subject. Numerous methods have been used to assist managers in making investment decisions. This chapter describes techniques other than the net present value method and evaluates their strengths and weaknesses. The need to separate the financing decision from the investment decision is explored in greater depth and the process useful for evaluating leases is presented.

CHAPTER HIGHLIGHTS

A. The net present value (NPV) method using the cost of capital as the discount rate is the most conceptually sound approach to investment decisions. Methods that do not consider the time value of money are inferior.

B. One limitation of the NPV approach is that the amount of investment is ignored. One variation of the NPV method that considers the size of the investment is the internal rate of return.

C. The **internal rate of return**, IRR, (also called the time-adjusted rate of return) is used to determine the true rate of return on the project. The analyst does not need to know the cost of capital to use this technique.

D. However, the net present value is superior to the internal rate of return for the following reasons: (1) it is a single ranking measure, and (2) it results in a better ranking of alternatives. It is also a better decision model when mutually exclusive projects are being evaluated. The NPV assumes that the company can reinvest its idle cash in a project which will cover its cost of capital. The IRR method does not consider investing idle cash. The scale effect refers to ignoring the amount of funds that can be invested at a given rate. Finally, the NPV is superior in analyzing projects with different lives because it assumes funds that are available at the end of one project are reinvested in another that covers its cost of capital.

E. The **excess present value index** indicates the number of present value dollars generated per dollar of investment. In absence of mutually exclusive projects, the NPV and the excess present value will result in the same accept/reject decisions. Otherwise, the rankings may be different.

F. A method often used to evaluate investment projects is the **payback** method. The payback period is the time it takes for the original investment to be repaid. It ignores the time value of money but is used because of its simplicity.

G. To take the time value of money into consideration, the **discounted payback method** has been suggested. This method is similar to the ordinary payback method but it defines time as the period that elapsed before the present value of the cumulative net cash flows equals the initial cash outlay.

H. A very popular method used to analyze investments is the **accounting rate of return**. The accounting rate of return method is also referred to as the rate of **return on investment** (ROI). While ROI could define investment as the stockholder's equity in the business, in this context the investment is the purchase of an asset. In calculating the asset's ROI, accounting income is used. ROI is computed by dividing the average yearly income from the project (accrual accounting income) by the average investment in the project (often measured in terms of book value). The calculation ignores the time value of money as well as cash flows. However, it is easy to measure and many managers are evaluated on their ability to meet a target ROI.

I. Investment decisions should not be dependent on financing decisions. If a project can earn a return at least equal to the firm's cost of capital, it should be accepted. As long as a company does not borrow at a rate which is higher than its before tax cost of capital (otherwise it would not be profitable), any investment undertaken that covers its cost of capital will improve the overall performance of the firm.

J. Leasing is a form of financing. Managers must first decide whether a leasing investment is desirable (assuming it could be purchased immediately for cash), then they should evaluate the lease terms. Managers usually have a choice of financing the equipment through the leasing company or using other financial institutions.

M. Leverage occurs when the rate of return on total capital is increased as a result of using borrowed funds.

SELF-TEST AND PRACTICE EXERCISES

A. **MATCHING**

Match each of the terms with its meaning.

Term	Meaning
___1. Payback period	a. Decision about the way assets are financed.
___2. Leverage	b. The length of time that elapses before the investment can be returned.
___3. Accounting rate of return	c. Selecting from alternative, acceptable projects.
___4. Excess present value index	d. The discount rate that equates the net present value of a stream of cash outflows and inflows to zero.
___5. Internal rate of return	e. Income for a period divided by the average investment during the period.
___6. Scale effect	f. Income for a period divided by average investment during the period.
___7. Financing decision	g. The effect that ignores the amount of funds invested during the period.
___8. Investment decision	h. Present value of future cash flows divided by the initial investment.

B. ALTERNATIVES TO NET PRESENT VALUE

The ABC Company is evaluating a capital-budgeting proposal for the current year. The relevant data is given below:

Year	Present Value of an Annuity In Arrears of $1 at 15%
1	.870
2	1.626
3	2.284
4	2.856
5	3.353
6	3.785

The initial investment would be $30,000. It would be depreciated on a straight-line basis over six years with no salvage value. The before-tax annual cash inflow due to this investment is $10,000, and the income tax rate is 40% paid the same year as incurred. The desired rate of return is 15%. All cash flows occur at year end.

REQUIRED:

1. What is the after-tax accounting rate of return on ABC's capital-budgeting proposal?

2. What is the after-tax payback for ABC's capital-budgeting proposal?

3. What is the net present value of ABC's capital-budgeting proposal?

C. RANKING ALTERNATIVE INVESMENTS

Each of the two projects requires an investment of $800 in equipment. The firm's cost of capital is 10%. The cash flow patterns and residual (cash) value of equipment are as follows:

	Cash Flows		Residual Value	
Year-end	A	B	A	B
1	$400	$100	$400	$650
2	400	200	140	550
3	200	200	100	520
4	100	200	-0-	400
5	-0-	300		200
6		400		-0-

REQUIRED:

1. Calculate the present value and net present value of each project at each of the following costs of capital: 0, 10, and 20 percent.

2. Rank the investments by the following methods:

   a. Payback
   b. Internal rate of return
   c. Net present value at cost of capital at 10 percent
   d. Excess present value index, at a cost of capital at 10%

Complete the chart below:

	A	B	Choice
a. Payback	_____	_____	_____
b. Internal rate of return	_____	_____	_____
c. Net present value	_____	_____	_____
d. Excess present value index	_____	_____	_____

D. LEASE DECISION

The Tamar Company is considering whether to acquire a new piece of equipment that has a 4-year life. The equipment costs $10,000 and will generate net cash flows of $5,000 the first year, $4,500 the second year, $4,000 the third year and $3,000 the fourth year. The manufacturer is willing to lease the asset for four years on a non-cancelable basis (that is, on the basis that Tamar Company must make payments for the four years no matter what happens). The annual lease payments would be $3,019 per year. If the company borrows from the bank at 8%, the following payments would be made:

Year-end Payments

	Interest		Principal		Total
1	$800	+	$2,219	=	$3,019
2	622	+	2,397	=	3,019
3	431	+	2,588	=	3,019
4	223	+	2,796	=	3,019

The income tax rate is 40%. The company's after-tax cost of capital is 10%.

REQUIRED:

1. Should the company acquire the asset? Complete the chart below:

	1	2	3	4	Total
Pretax cash inflows less cash outflow expenses	_____	_____	_____	_____	_____
Depreciation	_____	_____	_____	_____	_____
Pretax income	_____	_____	_____	_____	_____
Income tax expense	_____	_____	_____	_____	_____
Net cash flow	_____	_____	_____	_____	_____
Discount factor	_____	_____	_____	_____	
Present value of cash flow	_____	_____	_____	_____	_____
Cost of asset					_____
Net present value					_____

2. What is the present value of the net cash flows if the company leases? Complete the chart below:

	1	2	3	4	Total
Pretax cash inflows less cash outflow expense	_____	_____	_____	_____	_____
Lease payments	_____	_____	_____	_____	_____
Pretax income	_____	_____	_____	_____	_____
Income tax expense	_____	_____	_____	_____	_____
Net cash flow	_____	_____	_____	_____	_____
Discount factor	_____	_____	_____	_____	
Present value of cash flow	_____	_____	_____	_____	_____

3. What is the present value of the net cash flows if the company buys?

	1	2	3	4	Total
Pretax cash inflows less cash outflow expense					
Depreciation					
Interest expense					
Pretax income					
Income tax expense					
Principal payment					
Net cash flow					
Discount factor					
Present value of cash flow					

4. Should the company lease or buy? _____

SOLUTIONS

A. MATCHING:

    1. b   2. e   3. f   4. h

    5. d   6. g   7. a   8. c

B. ALTERNATIVES TO NET PRESENT VALUE:

    1. Net income before depreciation $10,000
       Less depreciation ($30,000/6)   5,000
       Net income before tax $ 5,000
       Income taxes (40%)   2,000
       Net income after tax $ 3,000

Average investment:
  Beginning of Year 1 $30,000
  End of Year 6   0
  Average   15,000

$$\frac{\text{Net Income After Tax}}{\text{Average Investment}} = \frac{\$3,000}{\$15,000} = 20\%$$

2. Cash income before depreciation $10,000
   Less taxes   2,000
   Cash income after taxes $ 8,000

$$\frac{\text{Investment}}{\text{Annual cash inflow}} = \frac{\$30,000}{\$8,000} = 3.75 \text{ years}$$

3. PV of $8,000 for 6 years = $8,000 (3.785) = $30,280
   Less cost of asset   30,000
   Net present value $ 280

C. RANKING ALTERNATIVE INVESTMENTS:

   1. At 0%:

Year	Interest factor	A	B
1	1.0	400	100
2	1.0	400	200
3	1.0	200	200
4	1.0	100	200
5	1.0		300
6	1.0		400
Present value		1,100	1,400
Less cost of asset		800	800
Net present value		300	600

At 10%

Year	Interest factor	A	B
1	0.909	364	91
2	0.826	330	165
3	0.751	150	150
4	0.683	68	137
5	0.621		186
6	0.564		226
Present value		912	955
Less cost of asset		800	800
Net present value		112	155

At 20%

Year	Interest factor	A	B
1	0.833	333	83
2	0.694	278	139
3	0.579	116	116
4	0.482	48	96
5	0.402		121
6	0.335		134
Present value		775	689
Less cost of asset		800	800
Net present value		25	111

2.

	A	B	Choice
a. Payback	2 yrs.	4 1/3 yrs.	A
b. Internal rate of return	18%	15 1/4%	A
c. Net present value	$112	$155	B
d. Excess present value index	.14	.19	B

D. LEASE DECISION:

1. Yes, the company should acquire the asset. The net present value is positive:

	1	2	3	4	Total
Pretax cash inflows less cash outflow expenses	$5,000	$4,500	$4,000	$3,000	$16,500
Depreciation	2,500	2,500	2,500	2,500	10,000
Pretax income	2,500	2,000	1,500	500	6,500
Income tax expense	1,000	800	600	200	2,600
Net cash flow	4,000	3,700	3,400	2,800	13,900
Discount factor	.909	.826	.751	.683	
Present value of cash flow	3,636	3,056	2,553	1,912	11,157
Cost of asset					10,000
Net present value					1,157

2. The present value of the net cash flows if the company leases:

	1	2	3	4	Total
Pretax cash inflows less cash outflow expense	$5,000	$4,500	$4,000	$3,000	$16,500
Lease payments	3,019	3,019	3,019	3,019	12,076
Pretax income	1,981	1,481	981	(19)	4,424
Income tax expense	792	592	392	(8)	1,768
Net cash flow	1,189	889	589	(11)	2,656
Discount factor	.909	.826	.751	.683	
Present value of cash flow	1,081	734	442	(8)	2,249

3. The present value of the net cash flows if the company buys:

	1	2	3	4	Total
Pretax cash inflows less cash outflow expense	$5,000	$4,500	$4,000	$3,000	$16,500
Depreciation	2,500	2,500	2,500	2,500	10,000
Interest expense	800	622	431	223	2,076
Pretax income	1,700	1,378	1,069	277	4,424
Income tax expense	680	551	428	111	1,170
Principal payment	2,219	2,397	2,588	2,796	10,000
Net cash flow	1,301	930	553	(130)	2,654
Discount factor	.909	.826	.751	.683	
Present value of cash flow	1,183	768	415	(89)	2,277

4. The company should purchase the asset.

STUDY PLAN

1. Review Problem 2 for Self-Study carefully. The subject of capital budgeting is one of the most difficult to master.

2. Study Exhibit 10.7 in the text. Redo the exercise assuming the discount rate is 8%. Should the company acquire the asset? Should the company lease the asset? Check your solution with the answer on the next page. This is another good application for an electronic spreadsheet.

3. Review the following outline.

REVIEW OUTLINE

I. Alternatives to net present value for evaluating projects.

   A. The excess present value index is computed as the ratio of the present value of future cash flows to the initial investment. It indicates the number of present dollars generated per dollar of investment.

SOLUTION TO EXHIBIT 10.7 (IN TEXT)
DISCOUNT RATE CHANGED TO 8%

PURCHASE ASSET OUTRIGHT: NO BORROWING

END OF YEAR	PRETAX CASH INFLOWS MINUS CASH OUTFLOWS EXPENSES	DEPRECIATION	LEASE PAYMENTS	PRETAX INCOME	INCOME TAX EXPENSE	NET CASH INFLOWS (OUTFLOWS)	PRESENT VALUE OF NET CASH FLOWS
0	(100,000)					(100,000)	(100,000)
1	50,000	20,000		30,000	12,000	38,000	35,185
2	40,000	20,000		20,000	8,000	32,000	27,435
3	30,000	20,000		10,000	4,000	26,000	20,640
4	25,000	20,000		5,000	2,000	23,000	16,906
5	15,000	20,000		(5,000)	(2,000)	17,000	11,570
Totals	60,000	100,000		60,000	24,000	36,000	11,735

LEASE ASSET: LEASE PAYMENT MADE AT THE END OF EACH PERIOD

END OF YEAR	PRETAX CASH INFLOWS MINUS CASH OUTFLOWS EXPENSES	DEPRECIATION	LEASE PAYMENTS	PRETAX INCOME	INCOME TAX EXPENSE	NET CASH INFLOWS (OUTFLOWS)	PRESENT VALUE OF NET CASH FLOWS
0							
1	50,000		29,832	20,168	8,067	12,101	11,205
2	40,000		29,832	10,168	4,067	6,101	5,231
3	30,000		29,832	168	67	101	80
4	25,000		29,832	(4,832)	(1,933)	(2,899)	(2,131)
5	15,000		29,829	(14,829)	(5,932)	(8,897)	(6,055)
Totals	160,000		149,158	10,843	4,336	6,507	8,330

ANSWER: Since the net present value of purchasing is $11,735, the asset should be acquired. However, the net present value of leasing, $8,330, is less than the net present value of purchasing. Thus, the asset should not be leased.

B. The internal rate of return (or time-adjusted rate of return) of a project is the discount rate equating the present value of all cash inflows and outflows to zero.

   1. The NPV is superior to the IRR due to:

      (1) its single ranking measure and

      (2) better ranking of alternatives.

   2. It suffers from several deficiencies:

      a. Analysis of projects with different lives.

      b. Ignores the scale effect (the amount of funds invested).

      c. Ignores the fact that idle funds invested must be invested at the cost of capital.

C. Payback.

   1. Ignores the time value of money.

   2. Only projects that accumulate cash inflows equals to the initial investment within a designated cutoff time are accepted. Ignores cash inflows after this date.

D. Discounted payback.

   1. Considers the time value of money.

   2. Only projects that accumulate discounted cash flows equal to the initial investment within a designated cutoff time are accepted. Ignores cash flows after this date.

E. Accounting rate of return.

   1. Ignores the time value of money.

   2. Is defined as the average yearly income from the project divided by the average investment in the project.

   3. Suffers from accrual accounting alternatives affecting profit calculations and declining asset values due to depreciation charges.

II. Separation of investment and financing.

   A. All investment decisions should be made separate from financing decisions.

   B. Lease decisions should be made following the same steps as a purchase.

      1. Investment. Determine the net present value of the cash flows generated by the asset using the firm's cost of capital assuming it was purchased for cash.

      2. Financing. Calculate the net present value of the lease payments, discounting at the firm's cost of capital. Next, determine the net present value of borrowing using the firm's cost of capital in computing discount factors. Firms can usually choose between lease financing and traditional financing.

CHAPTER 11

PLANNING, CONTROL, AND INCENTIVES

This is the first of four chapters that are concerned with the second major use of managerial accounting information, managerial planning, control and performance evaluation. This chapter presents an overview of the planning and control process. Criteria are examined for developing good planning and control systems, including assigning responsibility for activities to responsibility centers, developing performance measurements, and setting standards. The impact of the system on employee motivation and performance is discussed.

CHAPTER HIGHLIGHTS

A. The purpose of the **planning and control process** is to plan how to use all the resources of the company to achieve specific goals and to control the use of the firm's resources. While external accounting reports focus on only assets that meet specified criteria, managers must consider people one of their most important resources.

B. The planning and control process includes the following steps: setting organizational goals, developing a strategic plan, planning for operating performance, comparing actual results with expected performance, evaluating performance and taking immediate corrective action and/or revising goals, plans, and future budgets.

C. Management must establish organizational goals (broad objectives) which will guide employees.

D. Management must develop a **strategic plan** which represents the method for achieving the organizational goals. Strategic plans include long-range forecasts of sales, costs, and financing arrangements.

E. The **capital budgeting process** includes (1) identifying opportunities for capital expenditures, (2) identifying alternative options and the results of each, (3) evaluating alternatives and making decisions, (4) preparing capital budgets, and (5) following-up and performance evaluation.

F. After the strategic plan is prepared and capacity decisions are made, management must develop a formal, short-term plan of action known as the **operating budget**. The operating budget is a quantitative plan of action for the year. All financial statements should be budgeted, but managers often focus on the profit plan (budgeted income statement).

G. The **feedback phase** is essential in the planning and control process. The feedback phase includes comparing actual results to budgeted expectations, evaluating performance and taking immediate corrective action and/or revising long-term goals. The feedback phase serves three purposes: (1) to motivate employees; (2) to guide corrective action; and (3) to help revise goals and plans.

H. Motivating employees is a complex task. It is necessary because principals have delegated responsibilities to their agents. Accounting information helps principals evaluate the performance of agents. Accounting performance measures have an enormous potential to affect employees' behavior.

I. When evaluating a planning and control system, ask: (1) what types of behavior does the system motivate?; and (2) is this behavior in the best interests of the organization? Planning and control systems should be designed to minimize conflicts.

J. **Goal congruence** is important to principals. Goal congruence occurs when all members of the organization assist in achieving the company's goals. Complete goal congruence is almost impossible.

K. Planning and control systems should make sense for the characteristics of the organization.

L. The measures used for evaluating performance should be relevant to the objectives or purposes of the responsibility centers. Often quantitative measures, other than dollars, are needed.

M. One problem in designing planning and control systems for some activities is that it is difficult to rely on quantitative measures for evaluating performance.

N. Performance measures should be informative about an employee's action. This should involve reporting performance relative to others in the organization.

O. In setting performance standards, two principal behavior concerns must be addressed: (1) the extent of employee participation in setting those standards and (2) the tightness of the standard.

P. A control system requires timely **feedback** if it is to be effective.

Q. Every accounting system must ultimately be evaluated in terms of its **benefits and costs**.

R. It is important to identify who is responsible for the activities of the firm. If responsibility is fixed, managers and other employees will know what is expected of them and they can be held accountable.

S. Planning and control systems are developed around **responsibility centers**. If an individual is only responsible for costs in a department, that department is referred to as a **cost center**. If a manager has control over only revenues, the area is considered a **revenue center**. Someone who has responsibility for both revenues and costs is working within a **profit center**. The manager who makes decisions about investments in assets as well as decisions about sales and costs is in charge of an **investment center**.

T. The key to fair evaluation of responsibility centers is to hold the manager accountable for only those elements that are under his or her control. It is also possible to evaluate the performance of the center separate from the manager. This can be accomplished by identifying those areas that are under the control of the manager compared to elements that are not under the manager's control but are important to the long-run profitability of the department or division.

U. There are three levels of planning and control systems: **operational, divisional, and organization-wide**. Operational systems deal with the day-to-day activities of the firm; divisional planning and control systems coordinate the activities of the operating units; organization-wide systems review the entire organization's activities.

V. Incentive compensation plans are designed to provide incentives for managers to achieve organizational objectives. While it is part of a total planning and control process, it often emphasizes short-run performance.

SELF-TEST AND PRACTICE EXERCISES

A. MATCHING

Match each of the following terms with its meaning.

Term	Meaning
___1. Responsibility center	a. A system for insuring that day-to-day activities are carried out according to plan.
___2. Cost center	b. The responsibility center that controls revenues, costs, and assets.
___3. Revenue center	c. The responsibility center that controls only costs.
___4. Profit center	d. The process of translating decisions into performance and evaluating how close performance coincides with expectations.
___5. Investment center	e. System that involves a periodic review of the company's activities.
___6. Planning and control process	f. A financial plan that is used to estimate the results of future operations.
___7. Budget	g. The responsibility center has control over both revenues and costs.
___8. Goal congruence	h. Centers of activity within a firm which have control and responsibility for an activity during a particular time.
___9. Operational control	i. When the individuals in the organization work to achieve the goals of the firm.
___10. Divisional control	j. The responsibility center has control over revenue only.
___11. Organization-wide control	k. Planning and control systems that focus on the performance of divisions.

B. PERFORMANCE EVALUATION

Assume your managerial accounting teacher indicated that the following policies were to be maintained in your class:

(1) Homework would never be graded, but you are required to do at least 3 hours of homework a night.

(2) Attendance does not count.

(3) Raising your hand in class at least 10 times, regardless of whether you know the correct answer, adds 10% to your grade.

(4) Your grade in the class will be determined by examinations, but, at this point, the number of examinations is not known. However, if the day is rainy, deduct 30% from your grade point average.

REQUIRED:

1. Comment on each of the four policies.

   _____
   _____
   _____
   _____

2. As a student, how would you react if the teacher asked for your input in arriving at a formula for determining your grade?

   _____
   _____

3. How does performance evaluation in a course compare to performance evaluation on a job?

   _____
   _____
   _____
   _____

C. PERFORMANCE EVALUATION IN GOVERNMENT

A local government agency is evaluated in terms of numbers of persons seeking assistance from the agency each month. Special privileges are awarded to the division that generates the highest increase in persons served each month.

REQUIRED:

1. What is the limitation of the performance measure?

2. What problems might emerge based on the need to continuously increase persons served in order to be rewarded?

SOLUTIONS

A. MATCHING:

1. h   2. c   3. j   4. g   5. b   6. d

7. f   8. i   9. a   10. k   11. e

B. PERFORMANCE EVALUATION IN A CLASSROOM:

1. (a) If homework was required, but never graded, only the students who have a personal desire to learn the subject would probably do the assignments.

   (b) If attendance does not count, many students would choose to spend their time in other activities.

   (c) If raising your hand in class at least 10 times, regardless of whether you know the correct answer, adds 10% to your grade, many students would gladly raise their hands.

   (d) If the grade is determined by an undetermined number of examinations, students most probably would become anxious. The uncertainty of when and how many exams would make many students uncomfortable. It is unfair to have grades dependent upon the weather.

2. Participation in setting standards often makes students feel that the system is fairer.

3. Performance evaluation in class is much like performance evaluation on the job. Employees want fair standards, know what is expected of them and want to be held accountable for only those areas that are under their control.

C. PERFORMANCE EVALUATION IN GOVERNMENT:

1. Measuring only numbers of persons ignores the quality of the service.

2. Requiring employees to constantly improve in order to get rewarded creates a situation that is nearly impossible to achieve. Morale will decrease and some employees may either leave the agency or fraudulently complete paperwork in order to meet their objectives.

STUDY PLAN

1. This chapter introduces many new terms and concepts. Review exhibits 11.1 and 11.2. in the text.

2. Try to answer at least one of the complex problems at the end of the chapter. Usually the solution is not hard to identify, but the implementation of change is often difficult and unsuccessful.

REVIEW OUTLINE

I. Components of the planning and control process.

  A. Setting goals and developing a strategic plan.

  B. Planning for capital expenditures.

  C. Planning for operating expenditures.

  D. Comparing actual to expected results.

  E. Evaluating performance.

  F. Taking immediate action and/or revising goals.

II. Criteria for evaluating planning and control systems.

    A. Planning and control design.

        1. Goal congruence.

        2. Benefits exceed costs.

    B. Planning and control of capital expenditures.

        1. Identification of opportunities for capital projects.

        2. Identification of alternative options.

        3. Evaluation of alternatives and decisions.

        4. Preparation of capital budgets.

        5. Follow-up and performance evaluation.

    C. Planning and control of operations.

        1. Development of the operating budget.

        2. Performance evaluation.

        3. Feedback.

    D. Evaluating performance.

        1. Dollar quantitative measures such as profits.

        2. Other quantitative measures such as number of customers.

    E. Fixing responsibility according to responsibility centers.

        1. Responsibility centers are units of activity within a firm which have control over and responsibility for an activity during a particular time. Often these are divided into:

            a. Cost centers, where the center has control over costs only;

            b. Revenue centers, where the center controls only revenue;

            c. Profit centers, in which the responsibility center has control over both revenues and costs; and

            d. Investment centers, in which the responsibility center has control over revenues, costs and assets.

2. Responsibility should be assigned so that a particular manager is held accountable for areas under his or her control only.

3. Responsibility centers should be defined in such a way that control over activities is based on a particular time period. Once capacity decisions are made, managers are locked into a particular level of fixed cost.

F. Performance standards are properly set.

1. Employee participation.

2. Tightness of standards.

G. Timely feedback.

III. Classification of planning and control systems.

A. Operational.

B. Divisional.

C. Organization-wide.

IV. Incentive systems.

A. Importance in total planning and control process.

B. Criticized because of its emphasis on short-run performance.

CHAPTER 12

OPERATING BUDGETS

Every business manager must consider explicitly or implicitly what the future will be like. An operating budget is simply a formal, quantitative statement of the management's objectives and a plan of action for the future. The principal uses of budgets are considered and detailed steps for developing a budget are presented. Operating budgets are useful for planning purposes, control purposes, and employee motivation.

The overall summary of management's plans for the planning period is known as the master budget. Once it is prepared and adopted, it becomes the major planning and control instrument. Major components include budgets for sales, production, purchases, selling and administrative expenses, cash flows, and the capital budget. Finally, management considers how all of these expenses will look when presented externally by preparing forecasted statements of income and retained earnings and balance sheets.

These budgets are normally prepared in detail for at least one year in the future. Often they are prepared in summary form for several years hence.

CHAPTER HIGHLIGHTS

A. Budgets are management's quantitative plan of action for the year. Budgets are tools which assist managers in **planning, controlling, and motivating employees**.

B. A budget requires managers to translate their plans into a formal, integrated plan of action. Generally, managers must agree on the one level of volume expected in order to coordinate all the activities of the firm. Thus, budgets are generally **static**.

C. As a tool for control, budgets serve as a criterion or standard against which operating performance is evaluated. When budgets are used together with centers of responsibility they can be very effective.

D. While budgets must be static in order for managers to plan, they should be adjusted to actual volume achieved whenever performance is being evaluated. Therefore, when budgets are used as a tool for control, they are usually **flexible**. That is, the amount allotted is adjusted to reflect what would have been budgeted for the actual volume achieved. Usually fixed costs do not change, but variable costs must be adjusted to actual activity levels.

E. Usually, if standards are set at levels that are challenging but perceived as reasonable, employees are likely to achieve targets. Thus, the budget can be a tool for employee motivation.

F. The **master budget**, sometimes called the comprehensive budget, covers all aspects of the operations of a firm for a year. It includes budgets for sales, production, purchases, selling and administrative expenses, cash flows, and the capital budget.

G. Steps to prepare the master budget include: (1) setting the organizational goals, developing the strategic plan and capital budgets; (2) creating the profit plan; and (3) predicting the financial position of the firm, its income based on generally accepted accounting principles and its changes in financial position for the next period.

H. To create the profit plan, the first step is to forecast sales. The sales budget is then based on input from various managers. This is the starting point for the profit plan.

I. Once sales levels have been predicted, the next step is to plan for inventories. Management must set target inventory levels for finished goods and raw materials. Units to be purchased or produced follow the following accounting formula: Units to be purchased (produced) = number of units to be sold (used) + units desired in ending inventory - units already in beginning inventory.

Based on the above equation, the **production** (purchase) budget can be prepared in terms of units to be produced (or bought) and the **purchase** budget, reflecting the dollars to be paid during the purchase budget period, can be completed.

J. The **budget for marketing and administrative costs** requires management to estimate the expected variable cost per unit and the total fixed costs to be spent during the planning period. Often marketing and administration costs include discretionary as well as committed fixed costs. In budgeting, it is helpful to separate these two types of fixed costs.

K. The profit plan is a budgeted income statement. It is helpful for management to present the information in two formats: one using the same principles as used in the financial statements (often full-absorption, accrual accounting) and another to reflect variable costing. The variable costing format is preferable for control and performance evaluation.

L. The key to comparing actual results with the master budget is to separate volume differences and cost differences. This is accomplished by using **flexible budgets**.

M. Performance reports that compare actual results expected to the budget should always show the direction of the variance as well as the dollar amount. A favorable variance has a positive effect on operating profits, an unfavorable variance has a negative effect. Managers should carefully evaluate the impact of these variances on the strategic and long-range goals of the company.

Actual performance should be compared to the flexible budget allocation that is calculated for the actual activity level achieved during the period. By doing so, differences due solely to changes in volume are separated from true cost differences.

Sales volume differences indicate the amount of costs that were saved (or spent) as a result of producing less (or more) than budgeted.

Purchasing, production, marketing, and administrative costs variances **reflect cost inefficiencies at the actual volume achieved**.

N. When production and sales volume are not equal, managers should be careful in analyzing the results. Since budgets incorporate a specified cost per unit (which is calculated based on a particular sales volume), differences in sales volume which affect production will have an impact on fixed costs per unit.

O. When any variance occurs, whether attributable to volume or costs, there are two alternative treatments to dispose of the difference. One method charges the full amount off to the period, the other pro-rates the variance among the affected accounts, inventories and cost of goods sold.

SELF-TEST AND PRACTICE EXERCISES

A. MATCHING

Match each of the following terms with its meaning.

Term	Meaning
___1. Static budget	a. Estimates of sales volume based on inputs from various managers.
___2. Flexible budget	b. A variance that decreases operating profits.
___3. Master budget	c. A budget that projects receipts and expenditures as a function of activity levels.
___4. Cash budget	d. A variance that increases operating profit.
___5. Sales budget	e. A plan that provides for specified amounts of expenditures and receipts that do not vary with activity levels.
___6. Sales volume variance	f. Summary of management's plans for a planning period.
___7. Favorable variance	g. It is based on the sales budget plus the estimates of desired ending inventory.
___8. Unfavorable variance	h. It shows the budgeted amounts for cash outflows and inflows.
___9. Pro-rated variance	i. A variance allocated between inventories and cost of goods sold.
___10. Production budget	j. A cost variance incurred as a result of actual activity achieved during the period differing from expected level of activity.

B. **PRODUCTION BUDGET**

Avery Corporation expects to sell 20,000 units of a finished product during the next year. The company began the year with 3,000 units of inventory and wishes to have 2,000 units of finished goods at the end of the year.

REQUIRED:

Prepare a production budget (in units).

C. **PURCHASE BUDGET**

The Avery Corporation in exercise B uses 3 units of raw material X in every finished unit. The company currently has 1,000 units of raw material X on hand and wishes to have 1,500 units in ending inventory. Each unit of X costs $3. (Use your answer in exercise B.)

REQUIRED:

Prepare a purchase budget for material X.

D. **SOLVING FOR CASH PAYMENTS**

The Olympiad Company purchases inventory on account from various suppliers. It normally pays 70% of these in the month purchased, 25% in the first month after purchase and the remaining 5% in the second month after purchase. Inventory purchased during the first 4 months were:

        January $25,000
        February   38,000
        March   20,000
        April   22,000

REQUIRED:

Prepare a schedule of budgeted cash payments to suppliers for April.

E. PREPARING BUDGETS AND DERIVING VARIANCES

Biofeed Products provided the following information about its 1985 results (the company uses FIFO):

	Actual	Master budget
Beginning inventory (200 units)		
Variable costs	$ 600	$ 600
Fixed costs	$1,000	$1,000
Current manufacturing costs (1,000 units actual, 1,200 units budgeted)		
Variable costs	$3,100	$3,600
Fixed costs	$4,900	$4,800
Ending inventory (100 actual, 300 budgeted)		
Variable costs	$ 310	$ 900
Fixed costs	$ 490	$1,200

REQUIRED:

1. Determine the budgeted cost of goods sold.

2. Determine the actual cost of goods sold.

3. Compute the sales volume variance.

4. Compute the manufacturing cost variance.

5. Complete the following chart:

	Actual results (_____ units)	Manufacturing variance	Flexible budget (_____ units)	Sales volume variance	Master budget (_____ units)
Variable costs	_____	_____	_____	_____	_____
Fixed costs	_____	_____	_____	_____	_____
Total costs	_____	_____	_____	_____	_____

6. The president argues the variances are not fully accounted for because the difference between the budgeted cost of goods sold and the actual cost of goods sold differs from the analysis in part 5. Reconcile the difference.

7. Management may choose to pro-rate the variances or write the variances off during the period. How would the income statement be affected if all variances were written off in the current period?

SOLUTIONS

A. MATCHING:

  1. e   2. c   3. f   4. h   5. a

  6. j   7. d   8. b   9. i   10. g

B. PRODUCTION BUDGET:

Target ending inventory	2,000	units
Expected sales	20,000	
Units needed	22,000	
Satisfied from beginning inventory	3,000	
Units to be produced	19,000	units

C. PURCHASE BUDGET:

Target ending inventory	1,500	units
Expected production (19,000 @ 3 units of X)	57,000	
Units of X needed	58,500	
Satisfied from beginning inventory	1,000	
Units to be purchased	57,500	units
Cost per unit	$3	
Purchase budget	$172,500	

D. SOLVING FOR CASH PAYMENTS:

From April purchases ($22,000 @ .70)	$15,400
From March purchases ($20,000 @ .25)	5,000
From February purchases ($38,000 @ .05)	1,900
Total cash paid for purchases	$22,300

E. PREPARING BUDGETS AND DERIVING VARIANCES:

  1. Budgeted cost of goods sold:

Beginning inventory	$ 1,600
Budgeted manufacturing costs	8,400
Budgeted goods available	$10,000
Less expected ending inventory (see below)	2,100
Budgeted cost of goods sold	$7,900

145

Calculation of expected ending inventory:

$$\frac{\text{Total budgeted costs}}{\text{Budgeted units produced}} = \frac{\$8,400}{1,200} = \$7.00 \text{ unit}$$

An alternative calculation of the cost of goods sold:

Units sold from beginning inventory (200 units)	$1,600
Units sold from current production (900 @ $7)	6,300
Cost of goods sold (budgeted)	$7,900

2. Actual cost of goods sold:

Beginning inventory	$1,600
Current manufacturing costs	8,000
Goods Available for sale	$9,600
Less ending inventory (see below)	800
Total cost of goods sold	$8,800

Calculation of ending inventory:

$$\frac{\text{Total current costs}}{\text{Current units produced}} = \frac{\$8,000}{1,000} = \$8.00 \text{ unit}$$

An alternative calculation of the cost of goods sold:

Units sold from beginning inventory (200 units)	$1,600
Units sold from current production (900 @ $8)	7,200
Total cost of goods sold (actual)	$8,800

3. Number of units not put into production   200 units
   Budgeted variable cost per unit $3
   Sales volume variance $600 Favorable

Note: The variance is favorable because dollars expected to be spent on variable costs were not spent. However, this reduction in costs is more than offset by revenues not generated as a result of reduced sales levels.

4.

	Actual	Flexible budget for actual	Variance
Variable costs	$3,100	$3,000	$100 U
Fixed costs	4,900	4,800	100 U
Total	$8,000	$7,800	$200 U

5.

	Actual results (1,000 units)	Manufacturing variance	Flexible budget (1,000 units)	Sales volume variance	Master budget (1,200 units)
Variable costs	$3,100	$100 U	$3,000	$600 F	$3,600
Fixed costs	4,900	100 U	4,800		4,800
Total costs	$8,000	$200 U	$7,800	$600 F	$8,400

6. From parts 1 and 2:

	From beginning inventory	From current production	Total
Budgeted cost of goods sold	$1,600	$6,300	$7,900
Actual cost of goods sold	1,600	7,200	8,800
Difference	$ -0-	$ 900 U	$ 900 U

From part 6:

Master budget	-0-	$8,400	$8,400
Actual results	-0-	8,000	8,000
Difference	-0-	$ 400 F	$ 400 F

147

The disparity between the two analyses can be explained by first breaking down the costs into their fixed and variable components:

	Actual	Budgeted	Difference
Variable cost	3.10	3.00	.10 U
Fixed cost per unit	4.90	4.00	.90 U
Total	8.00	7.00	1.00 U

Then, the following chart reconciles the two reports

	Cost of goods sold from current production (900 units)	Ending Inventory (100 units)	Units not produced (200 units)	Total
Master budget				
Variable costs	$2,700	$300	(1) 600	$3,600
Fixed costs	3,600	400	(2) 800	4,800
Total	$6,300	$700	$1,400	$8,400
Adjustment to master budget:				
Variable costs	90 U	10 U		100 U
Fixed costs due to spending too much	90 U	10 U		100 U
Fixed costs due to volume variance	720 U	80 U		(2)
Sales volume variance				600 F
Actual results	$7,200	$800		$8,000
Difference	$ 900 U			$ 400 F

(1) The sales volume variance is shown as an adjustment from the master budget in explaining the actual results.

(2) The fixed costs that would have been absorbed by the 200 units not produced is not considered in the managerial performance report but it does affect the cost of goods sold reported on the income statement.

7. If all variances were written off in the current period, none of the adjustments to the inventory cost would be allowed, instead, all of the $100 cost variances would be a period expense and the ending inventory costs would be only $700.

STUDY PLAN

1. The text Exercises 10, 11, 13 and 14 are similar to the study guide practice exercises. Try to do these first.

2. Next, try a comprehensive problem like Problem 30 in the text. Budgeting often takes up a lot of a manager's time. Your understanding of how all the parts fit together will help you in using budgets more effectively. Be sure to complete the problem by preparing a flexible budget and a performance report.

3. Review the following outline.

REVIEW OUTLINE

I. Managerial uses of budgets.

    A. Tool for planning.

    B. Tool for control.

    C. Tool for employee motivation.

II. The master budget.

    A. Is determined based on a specified sales volume.

    B. Components:

        1. Sales budget.

        2. Production budget.

        3. Purchases budget.

        4. Selling and administrative budget.

        5. Capital budget.

        6. Cash receipts and disbursements budget.

        7. Forecasted balance sheet, income statement, and changes in cash flows.

III. Flexible budgeting and performance evaluation.

   A. Flexible budgets adjust operating budget to actual activity levels achieved.

   B. For performance evaluation, managers should use a variable costing format.

   C. Income reported on external financial statements will differ from internal operating reports when volumes differ from budgeted production. Also, since various treatments to dispose of variances are possible, the reports may not be the same.

CHAPTER 13

MEASURING AND INTERPRETING VARIANCES

This chapter focuses on the feedback phase of the planning and control process. The feedback phase involves comparing the actual results achieved to budgets, evaluating performance, and revising goals, plans and budgets.

The use of variances is based on management by exception. It helps managers draw their attention to exceptions, or variances from expected. Quantifying variances and pinpointing responsibilities is the first step in variance analysis. Follow-up is necessary in order to understand why results differed from expectations.

CHAPTER HIGHLIGHTS

A. In variance analysis, pinpointing responsibility is crucial. Therefore, every attempt is made to isolate marketing, production, purchase, and administrative variances. While there are often interactions among responsibility centers, variances are first computed based on the center that is responsible for the cost or revenue.

B. Marketing is normally assigned responsibility for the sales volume, sales price, and marketing cost variance. The sales price variance is determined as follows: the actual quantity sold multiplied by the difference between the actual selling price and the standard selling price. The sales volume variance is determined as follows: the standard selling price multiplied by the difference between the actual quantity sold and the standard quantity sold. The marketing cost variance is determined by subtracting the flexible budget allowance for the actual activity achieved from the actual marketing expenses incurred for the period.

C. Administration costs are usually discretionary. Thus, the appropriate level of administration costs for the actual volume achieved is often difficult to determine. However, the administrative cost variance is calculated by subtracting the flexible allowance for actual level of activity achieved from the actual administrative expenses incurred during the period.

D. The purchasing department is held accountable for material price differences. Consistent with the concept of responsibility accounting, the price variance is calculated on the actual quantity purchased, not on materials consumed during the period.

E. The production department is held responsible for variable manufacturing cost variances, including direct materials, direct labor and variable overhead.

F. Variable manufacturing cost variances can be separated into their price and efficiency components. Graphically, this is depicted as:

Actual price per unit

Standard price per unit

Price variance	
Standard allowed quantity	Efficiency Variance

Standard allowed quantity for actual production   Actual quantity used

A shortcut formula approach is as follows:

Price variance: Actual quantity (Actual price - standard price)

Efficiency variance: Standard price (Actual quantity - Standard allowed quantity)

G. The variable manufacturing overhead variance is sometimes separated into two components: the **price variance** and the **efficiency variance**. However, the computation is dependent on the measure of the input activity, such as machine hours. Thus, variable manufacturing overhead variances should be interpreted with considerable care.

H. Fixed manufacturing cost variances for manufacturing purposes may simply have a price variance (rather than be divided into price and efficiency variances). The difference between the actual lump-sum costs and the budgeted lump-sum costs is known as the **price variance**.

I. Variance analysis is appropriate in manufacturing and non-manufacturing settings, such as service organizations.

SELF-TEST AND PRACTICE EXERCISES

A. MATCHING

Match each of the following terms with its meaning.

Term	Meaning
___1. Price variance	a. Standard selling price multiplied by the difference between the actual quantity sold and the standard quantity to be sold.
___2. Efficiency variance	b. Difference between fixed overhead budgeted for a period and the actual fixed overhead for that period.
___3. Standard cost allowed for actual activity	c. The quantity of inputs that should have been used in accordance with pre-set standards.
___4. Total marketing cost variance	d. Costs that can be altered at the option of management.
___5. Management by exception	e. A principle of management where attention is focused only on those departments whose performance is significantly different from that expected.
___6. Fixed overhead price variance	f. Standard price multiplied by the difference between actual quantity used and the standard allowed quantity.
___7. Control chart	g. Actual quantity multiplied by the difference between actual price and the standard price.
___8. Sales volume variance	h. The difference between the actual marketing expenses and the flexible budget allowance for the actual level of activity achieved.
___9. Discretionary costs	i. A quality control technique to assist managers in determining tolerable limits.

B. PRICE AND EFFICIENCY VARIANCES

The Fandbox Company produces sandboxes. Recently it established standard costs as follows:

   Material: 3 pieces per unit at $ .25 per piece.

   Labor: .75 hour per unit at $6.00 per hour.

In February, 3,000 pieces of material were purchased for $ .27 per piece. Two thousand five hundred pieces of material were used in producing 800 sandboxes. Labor costs were $3,355 for 550 hours worked.

REQUIRED:

1. Compute the materials price variance.

2. Compute the material efficiency variance.

3. Compute the labor price variance.

4. Compute the labor efficiency variance.

C. OVERHEAD VARIANCES

The following overhead data of the Jewell Company are presented for analysis of the variances from standard:

Forecast data (expected capacity)

Direct labor hours	20,000	
Estimated overhead:		
Fixed		$ 8,000
Variable		$15,000

Actual results:

Direct labor hours	18,600	
Overhead:		
Fixed		$ 8,060
Variable		$14,030

Allowed or standard hours for actual production, 18,500 hours.

REQUIRED:

1. Calculate the variable overhead spending variance.

2. Calculate the variable overhead efficiency variance.

3. Calculate the fixed overhead price variance.

SOLUTIONS

A. MATCHING:

   1. g 2. f 3. c 4. h 5. e

   6. b 7. i 8. a 9. d

B. MATERIALS AND LABOR VARIANCE:

   1. AQ (AP - SP)
      3,000 pieces ($ .27 - $ .25)
      $60 Unfavorable

   2. SP (AQ - SQ)
      Standard allowed for actual activity: 800 @ 3 pieces = 2,400
      Therefore, .25 (2,500 - 2,400) = 250 Unfavorable

   3. AQ (AP - SP)
      $3,355/550 hours = $6.10 labor costs per hour
      Therefore, 550 hours ($6.10 - $6.00) = $55 Unfavorable

   4. SP (AQ - SQ)
      Standard allowed for actual activity: 800 @ .75 hour = 600 hours
      Therefore, $6.00 (550 - 600) = $300 favorable

C. OVERHEAD VARIANCES:

   1. Actual expense - budgeted at actual volume
      $14,030 - $ .75 x 18,600
      $14,030 - $13,950
      $80 unfavorable

   2. (Actual labor hours - budgeted labor hours) x Standard rate
      (18,600 - 18,500) x $ .75
      $75 unfavorable

   3. Actual - budgeted
      $8,060 - $8,000
      $60 unfavorable

STUDY PLAN

1. The study guide exercises are like Exercises 11 and 22 in the text. Try to solve them.

2. Carefully review Exhibit 13.1 in the text. Compare it to the chart in Exhibit 13.9.

3. Review the following outline:

REVIEW OUTLINE

I. Variance calculations.

    A. Price variances. The difference between actual and standard price for actual quantity.

    B. Efficiency variances. The difference between actual quantity used and standard allowed quantity multiplied by the standard rate.

    C. Production cost variances:

        1. Direct materials price and efficiency.

        2. Direct labor price and efficiency.

        3. Variable overhead price and efficiency.

        4. Fixed overhead price.

    D. Marketing expense variances.

    E. Administrative expense variances.

II. The following chart is helpful in measuring variances:

	FLEXIBLE BUDGET	
<u>ACTUAL</u>	<u>FOR ACTUAL</u>	<u>APPLIED</u>

Direct Materials:

Actual quantity x Actual rate	Actual quantity x Standard price	Standard allowed quantity x Standard price
AQ x AP	AQ x SP	SQ x SP

$$AQ\ (AP - SP) \qquad\qquad SP\ (AQ \times SQ)$$

|———————————————|———————————————————|

Materials Price Variance   Materials Efficiency Variance

Direct Labor:

Actual hours x Actual rate	Actual hours x Standard rate	Standard allowed hours x Standard rate
AQ x AP	AQ x SP	SQ x SP

$$AQ\ (AP - SP) \qquad\qquad SP\ (AQ - SQ)$$

|———————————————|———————————————————|

Direct Labor Rate Variance   Direct Labor Efficiency Variance

Variable Overhead:

Actual hours x Actual rate	Actual hours x Standard rate	Standard allowed hours x Standard rate
AQ x AP	AQ x SP	SQ x SP

$$AQ\ (AP - SP) \qquad\qquad SP\ (AQ - SQ)$$

|———————————————|———————————————————|

Variable Overhead Rate Variance   Variable Overhead Efficiency Variance

Fixed Overhead:

Actual	Flexible budget

|———————————————————|

Price Variance

CHAPTER 14

MEASURING AND INTERPRETING VARIANCES: ADDITIONAL TOPICS

This chapter is an extension of the topics presented in chapters 12 and 13. Two modifications of the profit variance analysis and the cost variance analysis are presented. The fixed manufacturing cost production volume variance and mix variances are computed. The chapter also presents how to interpret variances under two situations: (1) when units produced do not equal units sold and (2) when materials purchased during the period do not equal materials used in production. The chapter concludes with a discussion of statistical models that help decision makers decide which variances should be investigated.

CHAPTER HIGHLIGHTS

1. In general, the difference between actual operating profit and flexible budget (expected profit at the actual volume of units achieved) is due to (1) a sales price variance, (2) marketing and administrative cost variances, and (3) purchasing and production variances.

2. When standards exist for input prices and quantities for each unit produced, variable cost variances can be further refined as either a price variance or an efficiency variance.

3. The fixed manufacturing cost variance was previously calculated as the difference between the lump-sum budgeted amount and the actual amount spent. However, companies frequently use a predetermined overhead rate to apply fixed costs to the units produced. As a result, the fixed manufacturing overhead results in a budgeted amount of fixed overhead per unit.

4. **The production volume variance** occurs when the amount applied to production using the predetermined overhead rate does not equal the budgeted lump-sum amount for fixed overhead. This can only occur when the production volume used to determine the denominator in the fixed overhead rate formula differs from the actual production volume. When the actual production equals the expected production, the production volume variance is zero.

5. The **price (spending) variance** for fixed manufacturing costs is the difference between the actual costs and the budgeted costs of the period. This occurs when the company spends more for fixed costs than was expected at the beginning of the budget period.

6. Previous variance analysis assumed that actual production volume equals sales volume. When actual production differs from sales, either inventory is

increasing or decreasing. Thus, one explanation for the difference in actual operating profits from expected must be the effect of the change in inventory.

7. If variable standard costs are used, and inventory changes during the period, the actual profits for the period must consider the variable costs assigned to both the beginning and ending inventory. However, variance analysis on the cost side is performed by comparing actual manufacturing costs for the volume achieved compared to the budgeted manufacturing costs for this volume. In this way, manufacturing cost variances are determined in the period the units were produced. The period in which the sale takes place is unimportant when considering the manufacturing cost variance.

8. In analyzing manufacturing cost variance, the method of disposing of the variance may have an impact on the overall explanation of differences in actual profit from expected profit. If the variances are charged to the period (through the cost of goods sold account), then the entire variance can be explained as a line item in a manager's report. If the manufacturing cost variances are prorated or allocated, some to inventory and the remainder to the cost of goods sold, then the amount of variance allocated to inventory must be separately identified as a component of the analysis. If inventory increases, some part of the variance will be deferred in the asset account.

9. It is important to understand the difference between full absorption costing and variable costing and to reconcile the profits reported under the two methods. Full absorption costing unitizes (determines the cost per unit) fixed costs and attaches those costs to the inventory, while variable costing treats the manufacturing fixed costs as a period expense. When inventory increases, full absorption costing will attach more costs to the ending inventory and report a lower cost of goods sold. If the cost of goods sold is lower under absorption costing, then operating profits will be higher. When inventory decreases, variable costing reports a higher profit because the inventory sold has a lower cost associated with it.

10. The difference between variable costing and full absorption costing can always be traced to the manufacturing fixed cost per unit that is assigned to inventory under the latter but not the former. The difference can be computed by multiplying the manufacturing fixed cost per unit by the change in the number of units in inventory. This conclusion assumes (1) the manufacturing costs are the same between periods and (2) manufacturing cost variances are charged off to the period rather than pro-rated.

11. Another complexity in variance analysis arises when direct materials purchased do not equal direct materials used. In this case, the materials price variance is calculated on the units purchased, while the materials efficiency variance is calculated on the materials used.

12. When a manufacturing process has the ability to substitute the quantity of various inputs that result in no apparent change in the product (such as eggs, flour, and sugar when baking a cake), then the material efficency variance can be misleading. A **mix variance** shows the impact on profits of using something other than the predetermined mix of inputs. This variance captures how much

the company saved or spent in comparison with what would have been spent using the predetermined mix. However, sometimes the change in the mix of inputs results in more or less output of the product. The impact of the change in output quantity is captured in the **yield variance**. Together the mix and yield variances make up the material efficency variance.

13. When confronted with variance reports, managers must decide which ones to investigate. Managers use a variety of methods to help them determine which variances need attention. One unsophisticated method is known as a "rule of thumb" in which the managers select any variance greater than a certain percentage. While this method emphasizes managerial judgment and is appropriate in many circumstances, some decision aids have been developed to assist managers.

14. One decision aid is the use of control charts. The variance is allowed to fluctuate within predetermined tolerance limits. Sometimes tolerance limits are set based on statistical confidence limits.

15. Control charts do not consider the costs and benefits of variance analysis. Decision models can incorporate probability analysis.

SELF-TEST AND PRACTICE EXERCISES

A. **MATCHING**

Match each of the terms with its meaning.

___1. Fixed overhead price

a. The additional cost (spending) variance of changing inputs in a production process.

___2. Fixed overhead production variance

b. A variance investigation method that incorporates costs and benefits.

___3. Mix variance

c. The difference between budgeted fixed costs and actual fixed costs.

___4. Yield variance

d. The savings due to increases in the output in a production process.

___5. Control chart

e. A variance investigation method that uses rules of thumb to establish tolerance limits.

___6. Decision models

f. The difference between applied fixed overhead and the flexible budget

B. OVERHEAD VARIANCES

Zeeman Company uses a predetermined rate for applying overhead costs to production. The rates for year 0 were as follows: variable, $3 per unit; fixed, $2 per unit. Actual overhead costs incurred were as follows: variable, $165,000; fixed $110,000. Zeeman expected to produce 60,000 units during the year, but produced only 50,000 units.

REQUIRED:

1) What was the amount of budgeted fixed overhead costs for the year?

2) What is the amount of under- or overapplied overhead for the year?

3) Compute the total variable overhead variance.

4) Compute the fixed overhead price (spending) variance.

5) Compute the fixed overhead production volume variance.

6) Compute the total fixed overhead variance.

7) Reconcile the amount in part 6 with the amounts in parts 4 and 5.

8) Reconcile the amount in part 2 with the amounts in parts 3 and 6.

C. OVERHEAD VARIANCE ANALYSIS -- NO VOLUME VARIANCE

Redo Exercise B assuming the volume was 60,000 units, the
actual variable costs were $185,000. There is no change in
the budgeted or actual fixed overhead.

REQUIRED:

1) What was the amount of budgeted fixed overhead costs for the year?

2) What is the amount of under- or overapplied overhead for the year?

3) Compute the total variable overhead variance.

4) Compute the fixed overhead price (spending) variance.

5) Compute the fixed overhead production volume variance.

6) Compute the total fixed overhead variance.

7) Reconcile the amount in part 6 with the amounts in parts 4 and 5.

8) Reconcile the amount in part 2 with the amounts in parts 3 and 6.

D. **MIX AND YIELD VARIANCES**

Grant Company makes a product, GC, from two materials: XX and YY. The standard prices and quantities are as follows:

	XX	YY
Price per pound	$4	$6
Pounds per unit of GC	5 pounds	10 pounds

In June, 10,000 units of GC were produced by the Grant Company with the following actual prices and quantities of the materials used:

	XX	YY
Price per pound	$4.10	$5.50
Pounds used	60,000	90,000

REQUIRED:

1. Compute the materials price variance.

2. Compute the mix variance.

3. Compute the efficiency variance.

SOLUTIONS

A. MATCHING:

1. c   2. f   3. a   4. d   5. e   6. b

B. OVERHEAD VARIANCES:

1. Budgeted fixed costs = $2 per unit x 60,000 units

    = $120,000

2. Applied overhead = ($2 x 50,000) + ($3 x 50,000)

    = $250,000

    Flexible budgeted overhead = $120,000 + ($3 x 50,000)

    = $270,000

    Over- or Underapplied = Actual - Applied

    = $275,000 - $250,000

    Underapplied = $25,000

3. Total variable   = Actual variable - Flexible (applied)
   production costs   budget costs   budget costs

    = $165,000 - ($3 x 50,000)

    = $15,000 unfavorable

4. Fixed overhead price = Actual - (Flexible) budget
   (spending) variance

    = $110,000 - $120,000

    = $10,000 favorable

5. Production volume variance = (Flexible) budget - Applied

    = $120,000 - ($2 x 50,000)

    = $20,000 unfavorable

6. Total fixed overhead variance = Actual - Applied

   = $110,000 - $100,000

   = $10,000 unfavorable

7. Total fixed overhead = Price variance + Production volume variance

   $10,000 U   = $10,000 F + $20,000 U

8. Total overhead variance = Fixed variance + Variable variance

   $25,000 U   = $10,000 U + $15,000 U

C. OVERHEAD VARIANCES:

1. Budgeted fixed costs = $2 per unit x 60,000 units

   = $120,000

2. Applied overhead   = ($2 x 60,000) + ($3 x 60,000)

   = $300,000

   Flexible budgeted overhead = $120,000 + ($3 x 60,000)

   = $300,000

   Over- or Underapplied   = Actual - Applied

   = $295,000 - $300,000

   = $5,000 overapplied

3. Total variable   = Actual variable - Flexible budget
   production costs   budget costs

   = $185,000 - ($3 x 60,000)

   = $5,000 unfavorable

4. Fixed overhead price = Actual - (Flexible) budget
   (spending) variance

   = $110,000 - $120,000

   = $10,000 favorable

5. Production volume variance = (Flexible) budget - Applied

    = $120,000 - ($2 \times 60,000)$

    = none (expected volume = actual volume)

6. Total fixed overhead variance = Actual - Applied

    = $110,000 - $120,000

    = $10,000 favorable

7. Total fixed overhead = Price variance + Production volume variance

    $10,000 F = $10,000 F + 0

8. Total overhead variance = Fixed variance + Variable variance

    $5,000 F = $10,000 F + $5,000 U

D. MIX AND YIELD VARIANCES:

1. Materials price variance = Price variance + Price variance
                               of XX   of YY

    XX = ($4 - $4.10)(60,000) = $6,000 U

    YY = ($6 - $5.50)(90,000) = $45,000 F

    Total = $39,000 F

2. Mix variance = (Standard price   -   (Standard price
                    x   x
                  {actual mix % x actual   {budgeted mix % x actual
                   total quantity})   total quantity})

167

STUDY PLAN

1. This chapter contains complex extensions of Chapters 12 and 13. To understand the difference between the materials price variance when materials purchased do not equal materials used, review Exhibit 14.9 in the text.

2. Operating profits will be reported differently using full absorption costing compared to variable costing when production does not equal sales because of the production volume variance. Review Exhibit 14.6 in the text to understnad why.

3. The decision to allocate variances to inventories and cost of goods sold or simply to write off the full amount to the period (through the cost of goods sold account) affects operating profits. Review Exhibit 14.7 to understand the alternatives.

4. Since fixed costs impact the cost per unit, the volume of activity must be monitored. The production volume variance provides feedback to managers on how well they predicted production activity. Redo the analysis in Exhibit 14.2 assuming the output was 70,000 units. Can you expain why the volume variance is zero?

5. Review the following outline.

REVIEW OUTLINE

I. Fixed manufacturing cost variances are due to:

   A. Spending too much (price variance).

   B. Estimating the volume of activity incorrectly (production volume variance).

II. When production volume does not equal sales volume, operating profits reported under full absorption costing will differ from variable costing.

   A. When inventory increases, full absorption costing will attach some fixed costs to the ending inventory valuation.

   The cost of goods sold will be lower and the operating profits will be higher.

   B. When inventory decreases, full absoprtion will release higher beginning inventory costs and the cost of goods sold will be higher. Thus, operating profits will be lower than under variable costing.

III. Disposition of variances.

   A. Management must decide how to dispose of variances.

   B. Variances may be prorated to inventories and cost of goods sold or written off in the period in which the variance occurred.

IV. Calculation of the materials price variance.

   A. Management may compute the price variance on the units purchased or on the units used.

   B. Price variances calculated at the time of purchase normally result in better control over materials cost.

V. Mix variances.

   A. When multiple inputs are needed for a particular output, a mix variance may be computed.

   B. The mix variance shows the impact on profits of using something other than the predetermined mix.

   C. The yield variance shows the impact on profits of obtaining a higher yield due to the change in mix.

   D. The materials efficiency variance can be broken into two components: the mix and the yield variances.

VI. Variance investigation models to determine which variances should be investigated, managers use:

   A. Rules of thumb.

   B. Control charts.

   C. Decision models.

CHAPTER 15

DIVISIONAL PERFORMANCE MEASUREMENT AND CONTROL

In this chapter, techniques for designing and implementing control systems for divisionalized firms are examined. There is no single "correct" way of measuring performance. With decentralized decision-making, there is a potential for conflict between decisions that are best for the division and decisions that are best for the firm as a whole. Each firm must determine how best to use performance measures that strike the balance between the advantages of decentralized, autonomous decision making and the actions of managers who make their own performance look good at the expense of the firm.

Performance measures for decentralized firms include divisional net income and divisional return on investment. Both of these measures require a definition and measurement of divisional revenues and divisional expenses. If sales are made between divisions, the company must determine the appropriate revenue to the selling division and cost to the buying division, that is, the transfer price. Bases for transfer prices include actual and standard cost of the selling division, external market prices, and prices negotiated between the divisions.

CHAPTER HIGHLIGHTS

A. Companies do not uniformly define the term **"division"**. In this text, the term division refers to a segment that conducts both production and marketing activities. A division may be either a profit center or an investment center.

B. Companies choose to **decentralize**, that is, delegate decision-making authority and responsibility because: (1) delegation allows local personnel to respond quickly to a changing environment, (2) frees top management from detailed operating decisions, (3) divides large complex problems into manageable pieces, (4) helps train managers and provides a basis for evaluating their decisions and (5) motivates employees.

C. However, decentralization has its disadvantages. Managers may not make decisions in the best interest of the company. Thus, one objective of decentralization is to create behavioral congruence or goal congruence.

D. In measuring divisional performance, the concept of divisional operating profits is commonly used. However, it does not consider the investment needed to generate the profits. To address this issue, return on investment, ROI, measured on divisional performance is calculated using the following formula:

$$\text{Divisional Return on Investment (ROI)} = \frac{\text{Divisional operating profit}}{\text{Divisional investment}}$$

$$= \frac{\text{Divisional revenues - Divisional operating costs}}{\text{Divisional investment}}$$

E. In cases where the output of one division is used by another division, a **transfer price** problem is created. The "price" assigned to the interdivisional transfer of goods or services represents revenue to one division and a cost to another. While the company as a whole is economically unaffected by the internal transfer price, performance measures of the divisions can be significantly affected.

F. There are several solutions to resolve transfer price problems: (1) direct top management intervention; (2) established transfer pricing procedures; and (3) negotiation among divisional managers.

G. Direct intervention allows top management to order a supplying division of the company to produce and transfer products to a buying division. Top management specifies the transfer price. This approach is time-consuming and reduces the effectiveness of decentralization.

H. Top management may establish rules for setting transfer prices. Usually, the transfer price will be the market price, but could be the product's differential cost plus its opportunity cost, its full cost, or a standard cost.

I. **Market price** refers to the price the selling division would receive if it sold its product outside the firm rather than internally to another division. It is an excellent choice for a transfer price because it represents the price the selling division would receive in an independent transaction. Thus, the selling division is not harmed. The buying division is free to go out into the market and find a better price or buy internally. In the case where there are cost savings by doing business inside the firm, the buying division could benefit from the lower charge.

J. When a selling division has unused capacity, it is normally to the firm's benefit for the buying division to purchase internally. With a market based transfer price, there is nothing to motivate the buying division manager to buy from another division. In this case, the manager of the selling division should consider **negotiating** a price.

K. The general rule for setting transfer prices incorporates the economic concept of **opportunity costs**. The buying division will make the optimum decision for the firm as a whole if the transfer price is determined by the sum of the differential costs to the selling division plus the implicit opportunity cost to the company if the goods are transferred internally.

If the product can be sold outside the firm, the opportunity cost is the profit foregone. If no market exists, the opportunity cost is zero. However, the opportunity cost must include any profits foregone from any possible alternative use of the facilities.

L. If market prices are unknown, many companies transfer the products internally at their **full cost, full cost plus a mark-up, standard cost** or **standard cost plus a mark-up**. Standards encourage selling divisions to be more efficient.

M. If one division exists solely to support the other divisions of the firm, treating it as a cost center is adequate to control and measure its performance.

N. **Dual transfer prices** are possible. The buying division could be charged with an amount different from the revenue credited to the selling division. This is appropriate when top management wishes to accomplish a specified goal.

O. Transfer prices based on differential costs represent a lower limit on the price the selling divisions are willing to accept. Market prices represent the upper limit buying divisions are willing to pay. Managers may negotiate prices anywhere within these two prices. Negotiated transfer prices are consistent with the concept of decentralized decision making, but it takes time and may lead to interdivisional hostility.

P. The key issue in measuring divisional operating costs is to understand how the following costs are treated: (1) controllable and noncontrollable direct operating costs; and (2) controllable and noncontrollable indirect operating costs. In general, direct operating costs, whether controllable or not, are always deducted from divisional revenues in measuring divisional operating profit. Indirect costs are charged depending on management's philosophy. Usually, controllable, indirect costs are charged at the market value of the services received. Noncontrollable, indirect expenses, such as financing expenses and income taxes, are sometimes charged to divisions so they understand the full cost of their operations to the company. In lieu of actual expenses, some companies charge their divisions with the division's implicit capital. Some arbitrariness occurs whenever indirect expenses are charged.

Q. When **return on investment** (ROI) is used to evaluate divisions, there are several issues in valuing the denominator of the ROI measure, specifically, what assets are to be included and at what valuation.

Assets to be included in the investment base should be those under the manager's control and defined consistently throughout the organization.

In assigning monetary value to the assets to be included in the investment base, managers can choose historic cost (net of depreciation or at gross book value) or replacement cost (net of replacement cost depreciation or at gross book value).

R. Managers should be careful not to focus on one single statistic like ROI in order to evaluate performance. Multiple performance measures, highlighting contribution margin, controllable operating profit margin, operating profit before interest and income taxes should receive attention. In addition, the impact of allocating the costs of the headquarters must be considered.

S. To assist managers in analyzing ROI, the measure can be disaggregated into the **profit margin percentage** and the **investment turnover rate**. As a result, managers can quickly focus in on the problem areas of the division by identifying its profit margin and investment turnover.

T. In establishing the minimum acceptable ROI for divisions, the risks associated with the operation must be considered. A problem associated with the measure is that it can discourage divisions from accepting projects that will increase the company's overall return on investment but bring down a division whose ROI is higher than average. To avoid this consequence, companies may evaluate divisions using **residual income**. Residual income charges a division for the company's cost of capital.

SELF-TEST AND PRACTICE EXERCISES

A. MATCHING

Match each of the following terms with its meaning.

Term	Meaning
___1. Transfer price	a. Amount charged for interest on the capital used by a division when no cash payments are really made by the division to the central corporate treasury.
___2. Decentralized decision making	b. Transfer prices fixed as a result of negotiations between the divisional managers involved in the transaction.
___3. Return on investment	c. A substitute for a market price used in responsibility accounting when one segment of the business "sells" to another segment.
___4. Residual income	d. Indicates the portion of each dollar of revenue that is in excess of the costs incurred.
___5. Cost-based transfer price	e. When decisions are made by the divisional managers for their own division.
___6. Market-based transfer price	f. Transfer prices based on actual costs.
___7. Negotiated transfer price	g. The ratio of net income to investment
___8. Profit margin	h. The ratio of sales to the investment.
___9. Investment turnover	i. The net income remaining after deducting an imputed "interest" charge for the divisional invested capital.
___10. Implicit divisional cost of capital	j. Transfer prices based on external competitive market prices.

B. INTRACOMPANY TRANSACTIONS

A divisonalized company has given you the following data:

	DIVISION A	DIVISON B	COMPANY
Sales	$100	$150	$250
Variable costs	60	70	130
Fixed costs	20	30	50
Total costs	$ 80	$100	$180
Operating profit	$ 20	$ 50	$ 70

Both divisions sell 100 units each. Division B is considering enhancing its product to include the product produced by Division A. Thus, it could buy all of Division A's output or buy the 100 units it needs from outside vendors. If Division B sold its products, including the enhancement, the selling price would be $250.

REQUIRED:

1. Prepare an income statement for the divisions and the company if Division B purchased the new parts from division A at the market price of $1 each. Is the company better off if division B enhances its product?

	DIVISION A	DIVISION B	COMPANY
Sales	_____	_____	_____
Variable costs	_____	_____	_____
Fixed costs	_____	_____	_____
Total costs	_____	_____	_____
Operating profits	_____	_____	_____

2. The manager of Division B feels the performance of the division would be improved if Division A would sell its product internally at its full cost. Prepare an income statement assuming Division A complied. What happens to the allocation of operating profit between the divisions?

	DIVISION A	DIVISION B	COMPANY
Sales	_____	_____	_____
Variable costs	_____	_____	_____
Fixed costs	_____	_____	_____
Total costs	_____	_____	_____
Operating profits	_____	_____	_____

3. Division A's manager feels it would be in the best long-run interest of the company if Division B buys from Division A. Therefore, the manager is suggesting that Division B buy all of Division A's output at a price of $110. Prepare a revised income statement. What happens to the allocation of operating profits under this method?

	DIVISION A	DIVISION B	COMPANY
Sales	_____	_____	_____
Variable costs	_____	_____	_____
Fixed costs	_____	_____	_____
Total costs	_____	_____	_____
Operating profits	_____	_____	_____

4. What conclusion can you come to concerning transfer prices in divisional organizations?

C. TRANSFER PRICES AND UNUSED CAPACITY

Newman Company has two decentralized divisions, X and Y. Division X has always purchased certain units from Division Y at $60 per unit. Division Y plans to increase its price to $80. Division X can continue to buy outside at a price of $60. Division Y's costs are:

        Y's variable cost $40
        Y's fixed cost $10,000

REQUIRED:

1. As manager of Division X, would you buy from Division Y?

2. Assume Division Y is having trouble selling its product for $80. Should top management require Division X to buy from Division Y?

D. ROI ANALYSIS

The following information summarized the operations of William Enterprises for 1985:

	Budget	Actual
Sales	$1,000,000	$1,200,000
Variable expenses	(400,000)	(456,000)
Fixed expenses	(500,000)	(600,000)
Income before taxes	$ 100,000	$ 144,000
Average total assets	$ 500,000	$ 800,000

REQUIRED:

Present a comparative analysis for budgeted and actual ROI that indicated that the ROI measure is a product of asset turnover and profit margin.

SOLUTIONS

A. MATCHING:

1. c   2. e   3. g   4. i   5. f

6. j   7. b   8. d   9. h   10. a

B. INTRACOMPANY TRANSACTIONS:

1.

	DIVISION A	DIVISION B	COMPANY
Sales	$100	$250	$350
Variable costs	60	170	230
Fixed costs	20	30	50
Total costs	$ 80	$200	$280
Operating profit	$ 20	$ 50	$ 70

The company would be in the same position if Division A sold its output to Division B or to outsiders. Division B's new product generates incremental revenues of $100 and the market price of its incremental cost is $100.

2.

	DIVISION A	DIVISION B	COMPANY
Sales	$ 80	$250	$330
Variable costs	60	150	210
Fixed costs	20	30	50
Total costs	$ 80	$180	$260
Operating profit	$ 0	$ 70	$ 70

All of the $70 profit is allocated to Division B.

3.

	DIVISION A	DIVISION B	COMPANY
Sales	$110	$250	$360
Variable costs	60	180	240
Fixed costs	20	30	50
Total costs	$ 80	$210	$290
Operating profit	$ 30	$ 40	$ 70

$30 profit is allocated to Division A, $40 profit is allocated to Division B.

4. Transfer prices affect the allocation of profits between divisions.

C. TRANSFER PRICES AND UNUSED CAPACITY:

1. No. If Division X is evaluated on operating profit, buying at $80 rather than $60 will reduce performance.

2. To improve the profit of the company as a whole, Division X should buy from Division Y because the incremental cost to produce a unit is only $40 as opposed to the cost to buy outside of $60. Thus, the company as a whole would be better off by $20 for each unit Division X buys from Division Y. However, if top management imposes a decision on the managers, hostility may be created. This might be a situation where dual transfer prices are acceptable.

D. ROI ANALYSIS:

	Budget	Actual
(a) Asset turnover	2.0	1.5
(b) Profit margin	10%	12%
ROI (a x b)	20%	18%

STUDY PLAN

1. Review the problems for self-study.

2. The exercises in the study guide are similar to Exercises 21 and 27. Try these next. Then try the exercises that incorporate adjustments to divisional contribution margin before computing the division's ROI, such as Exercise 23.

3. Review the following outline.

REVIEW OUTLINE

I. Divisional organization and performance.

   A. Advantages.

      1. Better decisions result from decision-makers who are close to the day-to-day activities.

      2. Divisional managers are better motivated if they are given responsibility.

      3. Experience gained by managers in running a division is valuable for the company as well as the manager.

   B. Disadvantages.

      1. Managers make decisions in their best interest, not the company's.

      2. Interdivisional competition may lead to hostility.

II. Return on investment (ROI) as the performance measure.

   A. Relates investment required to the profits generated.

   B. ROI is calculated as follows:

$$\text{Divisional return on investment (ROI)} = \frac{\text{Divisional net income}}{\text{Divisional investment}}$$

$$= \frac{\text{Divisional revenues - Divisional expenses}}{\text{Divisional investment}}$$

C. Measuring divisional revenues.

   1. Revenues are consistent with independent entities when all of the division's products are sold externally.

   2. When products are sold to other divisions, transfer prices must be established.

      a. Cost-based transfer prices.

         1. historic cost
         2. standard cost
         3. historic cost plus mark-up
         4. standard cost plus mark-up

      b. Market-based transfer prices.

         1. considers the opportunity cost to the firm
         2. provides a fair allocation of operating profits to divisions

      c. Negotiated transfer prices.

D. Measuring divisional expenses.

   1. Controllable and non-controllable direct expenses are charged to the division.

   2. Controllable indirect expenses are costs common to several divisions but controllable to a degree by any one division. Divisions are often charged for some part of this cost.

   3. Non-controllable indirect expenses are not traceable to, nor controllable by the division. These costs are arbitrarily charged, or not charged at all, to divisions.

   4. Special issues arise concerning financing and income tax expenses. Often divisions are charged an imputed cost of capital.

E. Measuring divisional investment.

   1. Assets included in the investment base are usually directly traceable to the division and controlled by the divisional manager.

   2. Valuation of assets in the investment base include historic cost, book value based on historic cost, replacement cost, and book value based on replacement cost.

III. Interpreting divisional ROI.

   1. Single versus multiple ROI's draw management attention to numerous ways of looking at performance.

   2. Residual income is an alternative to ROI. Divisions are charged for the implicit interest on capital based on the minimum desired rate of return that the divisions should generate.

   3. Disaggregating return on investments can be accomplished by separating the ROI into the profit margin percentage and the investment turnover ratio.

CHAPTER 16

SYNTHESIS: MANAGERIAL ACCOUNTING AND EXTERNAL REPORTING

The first fifteen chapters have focused on two principal uses of accounting information for managers: (1) decision-making; and (2) planning, control, and internal performance evaluation. Data appropriate for managers may be inappropriate for external users. A major portion of the lack of congruence between managerial and financial accounting is because management decisions are based on estimates of current and future cash flows. However, external reporting is focused on past cash flows and the allocation of those cash flows to periods of time in accordance with generally acceptable accounting principles.

When managers use accounting information to make decisions and to plan and control the activities of the company, they must be sure to select the correct format, elements, and valuations. This chapter brings many of the concepts introduced in earlier chapters into focus and applies them to comprehensive problems.

CHAPTER HIGHLIGHTS

A. Managers often need information in a different format including different elements and different valuations, than the traditional financial reporting system.

B. For decision making, managers must be concerned with what will happen in the future. A more reliable forecast often will help managers make better decisions.

C. Once the forecast is generated, managers make an operating plan, or budget, to communicate expectations to the entire organization. The budget is based on a specific level of output and therefore is considered static.

D. When performance is being evaluated, a flexible budget is prepared. The flexible budget compares actual results to standards that are adjusted for actual performance levels. The impact on volume variances are separately reported based on the lost or gained contribution margin on sales different from the units budgeted.

E. Performance reports should reflect the concept of responsibility accounting.

F. Comparison of actual costs to budgeted amounts provides feedback to managers. It allows them to make immediate corrections, or to revise their long-term goals and strategies.

G. In evaluating a lower-level manager or a division, the investment necessary to generate profits must be considered. In general, the historic cost of an asset is irrelevant. Managers should use current values whenever possible.

H. The time value of money is an important element in every business decision. Models that consider the time value of money are superior to those that ignore the timing of cash flows. Models that include a charge for the funds required help managers determine the impact of projects to the company's "bottom line".

I. External financial reporting and income tax accounting require the allocation of fixed costs to individual units of inventory produced. Such allocations for managerial purposes are likely to lead managers to incorrect internal decisions. Examples of contrasting uses of financial and managerial information are found in (1) static versus flexible budgets; (2) variable costing versus absorption costing; (3) ROI or residual income versus earnings per share; and (4) revenues versus receipts.

J. Using absorption costing for external reporting and variable costing for managerial purposes can cause significant differences in operating profits. Managers should understand the reasons for these differences.

SELF-TEST AND PRACTICE EXERCISES

A. IDENTIFYING CONCEPTS

Explain the meaning of the following concepts:

1. Decision-making
2. Planning and control
3. Responsibility accounting
4. Budgets
5. Standards
6. Flexible budgeting
7. Peformance evaluation
8. Controllable costs
9. Contribution margin
10. Full absorption costing
11. Variable costing
12. Variance analysis
13. Time-value of money
14. Cost of capital

B. **MATCHING**

Match each of the following cost terms with its meaning.

Term	Meaning

___1. Avoidable cost   a. Cost resulting from sharing facilities.

___2. Book cost   b. May be market value or replacement cost.

___3. Common cost   c. Cost that requires no allocation.

___4. Current cost   d. Differential cost.

___5. Direct cost   e. Actual exchange price.

___6. Fixed cost   f. Historical cost less depreciation.

___7. Historical cost   g. Escapable cost.

___8. Incremental cost   h. Cost that does not change as activity increases.

C. MATCHING

Match each of the following cost terms with its meaning.

Term	Meaning
___1. Indirect cost	a. A cost that needs to be allocated to cost objects.
___2. Inescapable cost	b. Costs that increase as activity increases.
___3. Marginal cost	c. Incremental cost.
___4. Out-of-pocket cost	d. Anticipated cost of producing a unit of output
___5. Standard cost	e. A cost that needs no allocation to a cost object.
___6. Sunk cost	f. Unavoidable cost.
___7. Traceable cost	g. Said of an expenditure usually paid for with cash.
___8. Variable cost cash	h. Cost already incurred in the past.

SOLUTIONS

A. IDENTIFYING CONCEPTS:

1. Begins with identifying a problem, specifying a goal, identifying alternative possibilities, gathering information about the alternatives, and concludes with a decision.

2. Specifies a goal or standard for actual performance, measures actual results, and reports variances from expected results.

3. Accounting for a business by considering various units as separate entities responsible for costs, revenues, profits, or investments

4. A quantitative plan of action for an operating period.

5. In total, same as a budget; at the unit level the anticipated cost of producing a unit of output.

6. A budget that projects receipts and expenditures as a function of activity levels.

7. Comparison of actual results to expectations.

8. Costs that can be influenced by the way in which operations are carried out.

9. Selling price less variable costs.

10. The generally acceptable method of costing that assigns all types of manufacturing costs to units produced.

11. This method of allocating costs assigns only variable manufacturing costs to products and treats fixed manufacturing costs as period expenses.

12. Separates variances into the price and efficiency components.

13. Recognizes that cash can be invested at a rate at least equal to a risk-free investment.

14. The average rate per year a company must pay for its equities.

B. MATCHING:

1. g 2. f 3. a 4. b

5. c 6. h 7. e 8. d

C. MATCHING:

   1. a 2. f 3. c 4. g 5. d 6. h 7. e 8. b

REVIEW OUTLINE

Since this chapter does not refer to a particular chapter in the text, no study plan is presented. The review outline summarizes the first fifteen chapters.

I. Part One: FUNDAMENTAL CONCEPTS

   A. Chapter 1: The Management Process and Accounting Information.

      1. Uses of accounting information.

         a. Managerial decision making.

         b. Managerial planning, control, and internal performance evaluation.

         c. Financial reporting and external performance evaluation by shareholders and creditors.

      2. Managerial accounting compared to financial accounting.

         a. Both are often consistent and complimentary.

         b. Differences attributable to GAAP vs. information needs of managers.

      3. Organizational environment.

         a. Controller is the chief accounting officer.

         b. Internal audit department provides auditing and consulting services.

         c. Treasurer is manager in charge of obtaining capital and managing cash.

      4. Professional environment.

         a. Accounting authorities generate standards and rules for external reporting.

         b. Certifications include certified public accountant and certified management accountant.

5. Costs and benefits of accounting.

   a. Users need information to make decisions.

   b. Generating information has costs and benefits.

B. Chapter 2: Cost Concepts and Behavior.

   1. Fundamental cost concepts.

      a. A cost is a sacrifice.

      b. The term cost is meaningful only if it is used in a particular context.

      c. Opportunity cost is the cost of using an asset in its best alternative use from the one being considered.

   2. General cost structure.

      a. Direct and indirect costs.

      b. Manufacturing and nonmanufacturing costs.

      c. Period and product costs.

   3. Cost concepts for managerial decision making.

      a. Cost behavior: fixed and variable costs.

         1. Basis for breakeven model.

         2. Concept of contribution margin useful in planning and control.

      b. Differential costs.

      c. Sunk costs.

II. Part Two: COST METHODS AND SYSTEMS

   A. Chapter 3: Product Costing Methods.

      1. Product costing for managerial purposes versus product costing for external financial reporting:

         a. Cost inclusion

            1. Full absorption costing

            2. Variable costing

         b. Cost measure

            1. Actual cost

            2. Normal cost

            3. Standard cost

         c. Overhead rates spread actual overhead costs to production.

      2. Choosing among alternatives

         a. Finer versus coarser

         b. Costs versus benefits

   B. Chapter 4: Accounting for Resource Flows: Cost Accumulation.

      1. Cost accumulation by department and cost allocation to products.

      2. Manufactured units include direct labor, direct materials, and manufacturing overhead costs.

      3. When overhead is allocated to the units produced through a predetermined overhead rate, it is called normal costing.

      4. Resource flows from raw materials, labor, and overhead to work-in-process to finished goods. Finished goods are ultimately sold.

      5. The basic accounting equation is beginning balance + transferred in = transferred out + ending balance.

      6. There are two types of costing systems: job costing and process costing.

C. Chapter 5: Cost Allocation.

1. Common costs must be allocated to some cost object such as units produced or departments.

2. The cost allocation process requires a selection of the cost allocation basis.

3. The allocation process can be performed by using the direct or step method.

4. Special allocation problems exist for joint and by-product accounting.

III. Part Three: MANAGERIAL DECISION MAKING

A. Chapter 6: Estimating Cost Behavior.

1. Types of costs:

   a. Fixed costs.

      1. Capacity costs.

      2. Discretionary costs.

   b. Variable costs.

2. Methods used to estimate costs:

   a. Engineering method.

   b. Account analysis.

   c. Using historic data:

      1. High-low.

      2. Visual curve-fitting.

      3. Regression analysis.

B. Chapter 7: Cost-Volume-Profit Analysis.

1. The model: Sales - Variable costs - Fixed costs = Profits

2. Assumptions:

    a. Plant capacity is fixed.

    b. Revenues and costs are linear.

    c. No change in productivity occurs.

3. Applications:

    a. Breakeven point.

    b. Sales volume necessary to achieve a target profit.

    c. What-if situations.

    d. Profit-volume graph.

    e. Multiple product lines.

    f. Contribution reporting.

C. Chapter 8: Short-Run Decisions and Differential Analysis

   1. The differential principle: the analysis of alternatives should be based on comparative benefits and costs of each alternative.

   2. Problems in identifying relevant costs.

   3. Applications:

       a. Pricing decisions.

       b. Make-or-buy decisions.

       c. Adding or dropping product lines.

       d. Product choice decisions.

       e. Inventory management.

D. Chapter 9: Long-Run Decisions and Capital Budgeting

   1. Investing and financing decisions are made considering the differential principles and the time value of money.

   2. Discounted cash flow methods adjust for the time value of money.

3. The net present value is an acceptable discounted cash flow technique. All cash flows are discounted to the present and the optimal decision is the one that maximizes net present value.

4. The cost of capital is an opportunity cost.

E. Chapter 10: Capital Budgeting: A Closer Look.

1. Alternatives for evaluating projects.

a. Excess net present value index.

b. Internal rate of return.

c. Payback period.

d. Discounted payback period.

e. Accounting rate of return.

2. Evaluating leases: separate financing and investing decisions.

IV. Part Four: MANAGERIAL PLANNING AND PERFORMANCE EVALUATION

A. Chapter 11: Planning, Control and Incentives.

1. Draws attention to translating decisions into action and evaluating actions to ensure that actual performance coincides with expected performance.

2. Criteria for good planning and control systems:

a. Objectives are clearly stated.

b. Responsibility is fixed according to responsibility centers. There are four types of responsibility centers:

1. Cost center.

2. Revenue center.

3. Profit center.

4. Investment center.

c. Employees motivated to help the organization achieve its goals (goal congruence).

d. Performance is measured against objectives.

   e. Feedback is timely.

   f. Benefits from the planning and control systems exceed costs.

B. Chapter 12: Operating Budgets.

   1. A quantitative plan of action.

   2. A tool for managers.

      a. As a planning tool, budgets force managers to integrate and coordinate all decisions.

      b. As a control tool, budgets provide a standard against which to compare and evaluate performance.

      c. As a tool for motivation, budgets establish performance criteria and goals to work towards.

   3. Master budget includes:

      a. Sales budget.

      b. Production budget.

      c. Purchase budget.

      d. Cash budget.

      e. Capital budget.

      f. Budgeted income statement.

      g. Budgeted statement of financial position.

      h. Budgeted statement of changes in financial position.

C. Chapter 13: Measuring and Interpreting Variances.

   1. Variance analysis reflects management by exception.

   2. Variances are often partitioned into price and efficiency components. The price variance is calculated on units purchased multiplied by the difference between the standard rate and the actual rate. The efficiency variance is calculated using the standard rate multiplied by the difference between the standard amount allowed and the actual usage.

D. Chapter 14: Measuring and Interpreting Variances: Additional Topics.

1. Fixed manufacturing cost variances are partitioned into price (spending) and production volume components. The volume variance results from inaccurate estimations of the volume used in the pre-determined fixed overhead rate.

2. When production volume does not equal sales, variable costing will present different operating profits when compared to full absorption costing.

3. Variance may be prorated to inventories or treated as a period expense.

4. When materials are purchased, the price variance is computed on units purchased.

5. Mix and yield variances may be computed when different inputs are substituted and/or yields change.

E. Chapter 15: Measuring and Interpreting Variances: Additional Topics.

1. Decentralization allows for delegation of authority and responsibility.

2. Special techniques are required for designing and implementing control systems in divisional firms.

3. Divisional performance measures provided by the information system include divisional net income, divisional return on investment and divisional residual income.

4. In decentralized firms, when divisions trade with each other, transfer price problems are created. Choices for transfer prices are:

    a. Market based.

    b. Cost based.

    c. Negotiated.

5. In measuring divisional return on investment, special problems are caused by allocating common costs, charging for the cost of capital and allocating income taxes.

6. In measuring divisional assets in the return on investment ratio, managers must determine which assets should be included and at what valuation.

CHAPTER 17

OVERVIEW OF FINANCIAL STATEMENTS

The results of a firm's business activities must be reported to individuals and entities outside the firm. Outsiders include owners, creditors, government agencies, labor unions, and others who are interested in financial information about the firm. In order to standardize information reported to outsiders, generally accepted accounting principles developed. Basic financial statements now include a Statement of Financial Position, Income Statement and Statement of Changes in Financial Position. This chapter presents the basic principles underlying these financial statements.

CHAPTER HIGHLIGHTS

A. Business enterprises must engage in financing, investing, and operating activities.

B. There are three principal financial statements: Statement of Financial Position (balance sheet), Income Statement, and Statement of Cash Flows.

C. The Statement of Financial Position presents the assets, liabilities, and equities of the company at a point in time. The balance sheet's basic equation is: Assets = Liabilities + Owners' Equity.

D. Recognition of what is an asset to be reported on the Statement of Financial Position and how it is to be valued follow generally accepted accounting principles. Assets are defined as resources that have the potential for providing a firm with future economic benefits.

E. Assets are generally valued at their acquisition or historical cost. However, some assets are measured at their current replacement cost, net realizable value or present discounted cash flow value. Assets are classified as either monetary or nonmonetary.

F. Monetary assets are assets that have a claim to a fixed amount of dollars. Cash, accounts receivable, and notes receivable are examples of monetary assets. These assets are usually valued at their net present value.

G. Nonmonetary assets are all other assets. Merchandise inventory, land, building, and equipment are examples of nonmonetary assets. These assets are valued initially at their acquisition costs and in the case of limited life assets, adjusted for depreciation.

H. Generally accepted accounting principles have developed from many underlying concepts and conventions. An important concept is that of going concern which assumes that the entity will remain in operation for a long time. This concept provides the basis for deferring costs and revenues to a future period.

I. Another principle of accounting is conservatism. It has been used to justify the nonrecognition of income until assets have been sold.

J. The objectivity principle requires accountants to obtain objective, verifiable evidence about transactions.

K. Assets are classified on the balance sheet according to the following categories: current assets, investment, property, plant, and equipment, and intangible assets.

L. Liabilities represent a firm's obligation to make a payment of cash, goods, or services in the future. Most liabilities are monetary and are valued at their discounted cash flow value.

M. Liabilities are classified on the balance sheet according to the following categories: current liabilities, long-term debt, and other long-term liabilities.

N. Owners' equity in a firm is a residual interest. That is, after the assets are sold and the firm's liabilities paid, what remains accrues to the owners. The owners' equity section of the balance sheet reflects the capital structure and accumulated earnings retained in the business.

O. The income statement is a measure of operating performance. Revenues and expenses are recognized according to accounting rules which follow either the accrual concept of accounting or the cash basis concept.

P. The accrual concept of accounting requires revenue to be recognized only when some critical event has occurred that is related to the earnings process. In addition, there must be good support that the transaction will result in cash being collected by the company. Under the accrual concept, expenses are matched to the period in which the associated revenue is collected. When expenses cannot be identified with a particular revenue stream, they are immediately expensed.

Q. The income statement might contain some or all of the following sections or categories: (1) income from continuing operations, (2) income, gains, and losses from discontinued operations, (4) adjustments for changes in accounting principles, (4) extraordinary gains and losses, and (5) earnings per share.

R. The statement of changes in cash flows focuses the reader's attention on the net cash flows relating to operating, investing and financing activities for a period of time. Since the balance sheet captures the firm's position only at one moment in time and the income statement reflects the operating performance of the company on the accrual basis, this third statement was developed to provide investors with useful information about the cash flows related to the operations, as well as the financing and investing activities of the firm.

S. All external reports must contain a note describing the company's significant accounting policies.

T. An important section of the external financial report is the opinion of the independent certified public accountant. The report contains the accountant's opinion as to the conformity of the financial statements with generally acceptable accounting principles.

U. The annual report to shareholders must include a discussion by management of the reasons for important changes in a firm's profitability, liquidity, and capital structure. Management must also comment on the impact of inflation on the firm.

SELF-TEST AND PRACTICE EXERCISES

A. **MATCHING**

Match each of the following terms with its meaning.

Term

___1. Current assets

___2. Monetary assets

___3. Working capital

___4. Intangibles

___5. Retained earnings

___6. Current liabilities

___7. Income from discontinued operations

___8. Extraordinary items

Meaning

a. An item that is unusual in nature, infrequently occurring, and material in amount.

b. Obligations of a firm that are due within one year of the balance sheet date.

c. Cash and other assets reasonably expected to be realized in cash, sold, or consumed during the next year.

d. Increase in net assets since the business was organized as a result of generating earnings in excess of dividend declarations.

e. Nonphysical assets such as patent rights.

f. Revenues and expenses related to a segment of a business which has been discontinued during the year.

g. The difference between current assets and current liabilities.

h. Assets that give rise to a claim of a fixed amount of dollars.

B. ACCOUNT CLASSIFICATION

Classify the following balance sheet accounts as (A) an asset, (L) a liability, or (E) an owners' equity account.

____1. Accounts payable

____2. Accounts receivable

____3. Advances from customers

____4. Bonds payable

____5. Cash

____6. Common stock

____7. Furniture and fixtures

____8. Income taxes payable

____9. Leasehold

___10. Notes payable

___11. Organization costs

___12. Patents

___13. Preferred stock

___14. Retained earnings

___15. Treasury shares

C. CASH AND ACCRUAL BASIS OF ACCOUNTING

Following is a three-year summary of the transactions of the Brooks Clothing Shop, which opened its doors on January 1, 1985 and went out of business on December 31, 1987.

1. Purchased furnishings, equipment, and display material on January 2, 1985 for $90,000, paid in cash. These assets have a three-year life with no salvage value at the end of their life.

2. Purchased merchandise and made payment on merchandise as follows:

	1985	1986	1987
Purchased	$210,000	$250,000	$220,000
Cash paid	180,000	240,000	260,000

3. Sold all of the merchandise each year at double the purchase price, with the following collections of cash:

	1985	1986	1987
Sales	$420,000	$500,000	$440,000
Cash received	310,000	550,000	500,000

4. Paid all other operating expenses, including salaries, in cash as follows: $80,000 in 1985; $110,000 in 1986; $180,000 in 1987.

REQUIRED:

1. Compute net income on the accrual basis and the cash basis for each year and for all three years in total. The equipment should be depreciated using straight-line for the accrual basis. Treat the cost of the equipment as an expense in the period purchased for the cash basis. Use the chart on the following page.

	1985	1986	1987	TOTAL

Accrual basis:

Cash basis:

2. Compare the two methods of computing net income.

SOLUTIONS

A. MATCHING:

1. c   2. h   3. g   4. e   5. d   6. b   7. f   8. a

B. ACCOUNT CLASSIFICATION:

1. L   9. A
2. A   10. L
3. L   11. A
4. L   12. A
5. A   13. E
6. E   14. E
7. A   15. E
8. L

C. CASH AND ACCRUAL BASES OF ACCOUNTING:

1. (000 omitted)

	1985	1986	1987	Total
Accrual basis:				
Sales revenue	$420	$500	$440	$1,360
Less: COGS	(210)	(250)	(220)	(680)
Depreciation	(30)	(30)	(30)	(90)
Oper. Exp.	(80)	(110)	(180)	(370)
Net income	$100	$110	$ 10	$ 220
Cash basis:				
Sales revenue	$ 310	$550	$500	$1,360
Less: COGS	(180)	(240)	(260)	(680)
Equipment	(90)			(90)
Oper. Exp.	(80)	(110)	(180)	(370)
Net income	$($40)	$200	$ 60	$ 220

2. The accrual basis of accounting reflects the going-concern principle which allows companies to recognize revenue prior to receiving cash as long as certain criteria are met. It also requires the deferral of expenses to a future period that will benefit from the expenditure. The cash basis gives the most conservative view because assets are expensed when purchased, instead of consumed.

STUDY PLAN

1. Review the concept of an asset in the text beginning on page 759. You should understand that acquiring an asset simply indicates a firm has more resources than before the transaction. It is possible that the firm has a related liability in the same amount and therefore, the net worth of the company has not changed. It is also possible that assets were acquired in exchange for an equity interest in the firm.
Income is recognized only when assets are acquired, and there is no related increase in liabilities or capital contribution. Try to solve Exercises 12 and 13.

2. The concept of an accounting liability is usually easy to understand. Check your knowledge by solving Exercises 14 and 15.

3. Income can be computed using the cash basis or the accrual concept of accounting. After reviewing Exercise C in the study guide, try Problem 18 in the text.

4. Financial statements usually follow a traditional format. Do Problem 20 to learn how the balance sheet and income statement figures are normally presented. Remember, dividends are a distribution of income and are not an expense of the company!

REVIEW OUTLINE

I. Primary financial statements.

   A. Statement of Financial Position: Presents a snapshot of the resources of the firm and claims on those resources at a specific moment in time.

   1. Elements.

      a. Assets: Resources that have the potential for providing a firm with future economic benefits.

      b. Liabilities: Represents a firm's obligations to make payments of cash, goods, or services in a reasonably definite amount, at a reasonably definite future time, as a result of benefits or services received currently or in the past.

      c. Equity: The residual interest of the owners in the net assets of the firm.

   2. Valuation.

      a. Monetary assets are valued at current cash or current cash equivalent.

      b. Nonmonetary assets are valued at acquisition cost adjusted downward for the cost of the asset's services which have been consumed or assigned to part periods.

      c. Liabilities are usually monetary and are valued at discounted cash flow value.

   3. Classification.

      a. Assets.

         1. Current assets: cash and other assets expected to be sold or consumed during the normal operating cycle of the business, usually one year.

2. Investments: Long-term investments in the securities of other organizations.

   3. Property, plant, and equipment: Includes tangible long-lived assets used in a firm's operations over a period of years and not generally acquired for resale.

   4. Intangible assets: Include patents, trademarks, franchises, and goodwill.

  b. Liabilities.

   1. Current liabilities: Obligations expected to be liquidated within the next operating cycle of the firm, usually one year.

   2. Long-term debts. Obligations due more than one year after the balance sheet date.

   3. Other long-term liabilities: Obligations not properly considered as current liabilities or long-term debt. Includes deferred income taxes and some deferred compensation obligations.

  c. Owners' Equity.

   1. Common Stock: Par value of firm's principal class of voting stock.

   2. Preferred Stock: Par value of firm's stock that has some preferences.

   3. Capital contributed in excess of par.

   4. Retained earnings: Earnings realized by firm in excess of dividends declared.

   5. Treasury shares: Cost of stock issued and bought back by the firm.

B. Income statement provides a measure of the earnings performance of a firm for some period of time.

 1. Accounting period convention: Usually one year.

 2. Basis for recognizing revenue and expenses:

  a. Cash basis of accounting. Revenues are recognized only when cash is received from customers. Expenses are reported in the period in which payment is made.

  b. Accrual basis of accounting: Revenues are recognized in the period in which they are earned. Expenses are matched to the period in which revenue is recognized.

 3. Classification.

  a. Income from continuing operations.

  b. Income, gains, and losses from discontinued operations.

  c. Adjustments for changes in accounting principles.

  d. Extraordinary gains and losses.

  e. Earnings per share.

C. Statement of Cash Flows reports the inflows, or sources, and outflows, or uses, of cash during a period of time.

 1. Used in assessing changes in the firm's liquidity and in the structure of the firm's assets and equities.

 2. Classifies cash flows based on operations, financing and investing activities.

D. Supporting schedules and notes.

 1. Summary of significant accounting policies.

 2. Auditor's opinion.

 3. Management's discussion and analysis of operations and financial position.

II. Underlying principles.

 A. Going concern.

 B. Objectivity.

 C. Conservatism.

CHAPTER 18

ANALYSIS OF FINANCIAL STATEMENTS

This is the second of two chapters discussing the analysis of financial statements. Such analysis is made to assess and interpret the results of past performance and financial position. It is helpful to external readers of financial statements, including stockholders, financial analysts, creditors and government regulators. In this chapter, financial ratios are introduced as a tool of financial analysis. Managers may use many of the same techniques in evaluating performance internally.

CHAPTER HIGHLIGHTS

A. Investments are made by investors who expect a return of not only their original capital but also a **return on their investment** that compensates them for the **risk** they accepted.

B. **Ratios** are useful tools of financial statement analysts because they summarize a lot of information in a form that is easily understood, interpreted, and compared.

C. Ratios computed for a firm at a given time can be compared to expected ratios for the same period, prior period ratios, ratios of similar firms in the same industry, or the average for the industry.

D. Some ratios focus on the income statement and are called **profitability ratios**.

E. The **rate of return on assets** is a measure for assessing a firm's performance in relation to the investment necessary to generate the profit achieved. It ignores the method of financing assets. The numerator is net income plus interest expense, net of income tax savings. The denominator is average total assets. To determine average total assets, many analysts simply use an average of the beginning and ending balance of total assets.

F. The rate of return on assets can be broken down into two component parts: **the profit margin ratio** and the **total asset turnover**. The analyst can then determine whether a problem exists because the profit margin on sales is inadequate or whether assets are not being used efficiently. The profit margin on sales is calculated by dividing the net income plus interest expense, net of income tax savings, by total revenues. The total asset turnover is calculated by dividing revenues by average total assets. Thus, the two ratios when multiplied determine the rate of return on assets.

G. The profit margin ratio can be analyzed further. Each element in the income statement can be described as a percentage of sales revenue. Thus, the analyst can focus on areas that have changed dramatically over the past several years.

H. The total asset turnover can also be refined. Since the total asset turnover depends on the specific asset management, the **accounts receivable turnover**, **inventory turnover**, and **fixed asset turnover** should be computed in order to understand the overall ratio.

I. The **accounts receivable turnover** is the rate accounts receivable are converted into cash. It is calculated by dividing net sales on account (credit sales) by the average accounts receivable balance. Normally, the more times receivables turn over, the quicker the company has cash from the sale to reinvest.

J. The **inventory turnover** captures how often inventory is sold. Since this is the first step in realizing cash from a sale, analysts consider this ratio very important. If inventory is too high, and not being sold quickly, often it must be sold at a markdown or written off completely. To compute the inventory turnover, the cost of goods sold is divided by average inventory.

K. The **fixed asset**, or **plant turnover** is a measure of the relationship between sales and the investment in plant assets. Some companies require investment in expensive machinery in order to generate a dollar of sales revenue. Other firms need very little investment to generate revenue. This ratio indicated how many dollars were invested in plant assets in order to produce a dollar of sales revenue. It is calculated by dividing sales by average plant assets.

L. One of the most important ratios for investors is the **rate of return on common stock equity**. Investors use this ratio to compare the rate of return on their investment in a particular company to alternative investments. To calculate the rate of return on common stock equity, the numerator includes net income less the share of corporate income that accrues to the preferred stock holders (dividends on preferred stock). The denominator is average stockholders' equity.

M. **Financial leverage**, or trading on the equity, refers to the ability of a company to finance operations with debt, earn an adequate return to not only cover the interest charge but also increase the rate of return to stockholders.

N. **Earnings per share of common stock** is calculated by dividing net income applicable to common shareholders by the average number of common shares outstanding during the period. Two calculations are made: one to reflect only the actual common shares issued and outstanding, the other to incorporate the result if all securities that could be converted to common were converted. The first ratio is called **primary earnings per share**, the second is **fully diluted earnings per share**.

O. The **price-earnings ratio** compares the market price of the stock with the earnings of the company. It is often expressed as a rate.

P. Investors are interested in understanding the risks associated with the investment. There are short-term measures of risk that capture the liquidity of the firm and long-term measures of risk that indicate the solvency, or capital structure, of the firm.

Q. **Short-term liquidity ratios** include the **current ratio** (current assets/current liabilities), **quick ratio** (cash, marketable securities, and accounts receivable/current liabilities), **operating cash flow to current liabilities**, and the **working capital turnover ratio**.

R. **Long-term solvency ratios** include the **long-term debt ratio** (total noncurrent liabilities/total noncurrent liabilities + stockholders' equity), **debt-equity ratio** (total liabilities/total liabilities + stockholders' equity), the **cash flow from operations to total liabilities ratio**, and **times interest charges earned** (net income before interest and income taxes/interest expense).

S. All ratios must be interpreted carefully. The valuations are based on accrual accounting concepts. There are interrelationships among ratios that must be considered. The analyst must be careful that the elements used are comparable across periods, firms, and industries.

SELF-TEST AND PRACTICE EXERCISES

A. **MATCHING**

Match each of the following terms with its meaning.

Term	Meaning
___1. Risk	a. Ability to meet debt when due.
___2. Profitability	b. A measure of variability of the return on investment.
___3. Liquidity	c. Capacity to earn revenues in excess of expenses.
___4. Solvency	d. The "nearness to cash" of a firm's assets.
___5. Leverage	e. The increased rate of return on owner's equity when an investment earns a return larger than the cost of debt financing.

B. **MATCHING**

Match each of the following ratios with its calculation.

Ratio		Calculation

___ 1. Return on Assets

a. $\dfrac{\text{Net sales on account}}{\text{Average accounts receivable}}$

___ 2. Profit Margin Ratio

b. $\dfrac{\text{Cost of goods sold}}{\text{Average inventory}}$

___ 3. Total Assets Turnover

c. $\dfrac{\text{Sales}}{\text{Average plant assets}}$

___ 4. Accounts Receivable Turnover

d. $\dfrac{\text{Net income before interest and income taxes}}{\text{Interest expense}}$

___ 5. Inventory Turnover

e. $\dfrac{\text{Current assets}}{\text{Current liabilities}}$

___ 6. Plant Asset Turnover

f. $\dfrac{\text{Total liabilities}}{\text{Total equities}}$

___ 7. Rate of Return on Common Stockholders' Equity

g. $\dfrac{\text{Net income + interest expense net of tax effects}}{\text{Revenues}}$

___ 8. Debt-Equity ratio

h. $\dfrac{\text{Revenues}}{\text{Average total assets}}$

___ 9. Current ratio

i. $\dfrac{\text{Net income - preferred stock dividends}}{\text{Average common shareholders' equity}}$

___ 10. Times Interest Charges Earned

j. $\dfrac{\text{Net income + interest expense, net of tax}}{\text{Average total assets}}$

C. **FINANCIAL RATIO ANALYSIS**

The financial statements for 1985 for the Marooth Company are presented below:

MAROOTH COMPANY

STATEMENT OF FINANCIAL POSITION

Assets	12/31/85	12/31/84
Cash	$ 20,000	$ 6,000
Accounts Receivable	40,000	60,000
Inventory	120,000	80,000
Property, Plant, & Equipment	200,000	207,000
Total Assets	$380,000	$353,000
Liabilities and Stockholders' Equity		
Current Liabilities	$ 80,000	$ 60,000
5% Mortgage Payable	160,000	162,000
Common Stock (30,000 shares)	120,000	120,000
Retained Earnings	20,000	11,000
Total Equities	$380,000	$353,000

MAROOTH COMPANY

INCOME STATEMENT

For the Year Ended December 31, 1985

Sales on account		$329,000
Less expenses:		
Cost of goods sold	$200,000	
Salary expense	60,000	
Depreciation exp.	7,000	
Interest expense	8,000	275,000
Income before taxes		54,000
Income Tax Expense (50%)		27,000
Net income		$ 27,000

REQUIRED:

Compute the following ratios for the Marooth Company for the year ending December 31, 1985.

1. Profit margin ratio
2. Total asset turnover
3. Rate of return on total assets
4. Rate of return on common stock equity
5. Earnings per share of common stock
6. Inventory turnover
7. Current ratio
8. Quick ratio
9. Accounts receivable turnover
10. Debt-equity ratio
11. Number of times interest charges earned

SOLUTIONS

A. MATCHING:

    1. b   2. c   3. d   4. a   5. e

B. MATCHING:

    1. j   2. g   3. h   4. a   5. b

    6. c   7. i   8. f   9. e   10. d

C. FINANCIAL RATIO ANALYSIS:

1. $\dfrac{27{,}000 + (8{,}000 \times .50)}{329{,}000} = 9.4\%$

2. $\dfrac{329{,}000}{(380{,}000 + 353{,}000)/2} = .898$

3. $\dfrac{27{,}000 + (8{,}000 \times .50)}{(380{,}000 + 353{,}000)/2} = 8.5\%$

    or 9.4% x .898 = 8.5%

4. $\dfrac{27{,}000}{(140{,}000 + 131{,}000)/2} = 19.9\%$

5. $\dfrac{27{,}000}{30{,}000} = \$.90$

6. $\dfrac{200{,}000}{(120{,}000 + 80{,}000)/2} = 2 \text{ times}$

7. $\dfrac{20{,}000 + 40{,}000 + 120{,}000}{80{,}000} = 2.25 \text{ to } 1$

8. $\dfrac{20{,}000 + 40{,}000}{80{,}000} = .75 \text{ to } 1$

9. $\dfrac{329{,}000}{(40{,}000 + 60{,}000)/2} = 6.58$

10. $\dfrac{80{,}000 + 160{,}000}{380{,}000} = .632 \text{ to } 1$

11. $\dfrac{54{,}000 + 8{,}000}{8{,}000} = 7.75 \text{ times}$

STUDY PLAN

1. Review Exhibit 18.11, Summary of Financial Statement Ratios.

2. After doing exercise C in the study guide, do Exercise 9 in the text.

3. Next try a comprehensive problem, like Problem 22 in the text.

4. Review the following outline.

REVIEW OUTLINE

I. Objectives of financial statement analysis.

    A. To assist stockholders in comparing alternative investment opportunities.

    B. To assist managers in pinpointing weak areas.

II. Usefulness of ratios.

    A. Ratios present a convenient summary, easily understood.

    B. By themselves, ratios are difficult to interpret.

III. Measures of profitability.

    A. Rate of return on total assets $= \dfrac{\text{Net income + Interest expense (net of tax)}}{\text{Average total assets}}$

        1. Profit margin on sales $= \dfrac{\text{Net income + Interest expense (net of tax)}}{\text{Revenues}}$

        2. Total asset turnover $= \dfrac{\text{Revenues}}{\text{Average total assets}}$

        3. Various expenses ratios $= \dfrac{\text{Various expenses}}{\text{Revenues}}$

        4. Accounts receivable turnover $= \dfrac{\text{Net sales on account}}{\text{Average accounts receivable}}$

5. Inventory turnover = $\dfrac{\text{Cost of goods sold}}{\text{Average inventory}}$

6. Plant asset turnover = $\dfrac{\text{Sales}}{\text{Average plant assets}}$

B. Rate of return on Common Stock Equity = $\dfrac{\text{Net income - Dividends on preferred stock}}{\text{Average common stockholders' equity}}$

   1. Earnings per share = $\dfrac{\text{Net income - Dividends on preferred stock}}{\text{Weighted average number of common stock outstanding}}$

      a. Primary earnings per share

      b. Fully diluted earnings per share

C. Measures of short-term liquidity.

   1. Current ratio = $\dfrac{\text{Current assets}}{\text{Current liabilities}}$

   2. Quick ratio = $\dfrac{\text{Highly liquid assets}}{\text{Current liabilities}}$

   3. Operating cash flow to current liabilities = $\dfrac{\text{Operating Cash Flows}}{\text{Current liabilities}}$

   4. Working capital turnover = $\dfrac{\text{Sales}}{\text{Average working capital}}$

D. Measures of long-term solvency.

   1. Equity ratios

      a. Debt-equity ratio = $\dfrac{\text{Total liabilities}}{\text{Total equities}}$

      b. Long-term debt ratio = $\dfrac{\text{Total noncurrent liabilities}}{\text{Total noncurrent liabilities + Stockholders' equity}}$

  2. Cash flow from operations $\dfrac{\text{Cash flow from operations}}{\text{Average total liabilities}}$
    to total liabilities =

  3. Interest coverage

    Times interest charges = $\dfrac{\text{Net income before interest and tax}}{\text{Interest expense}}$
     earned

IV. Limitations of ratio analysis.

 A. Ratios are based on financial statement data and therefore are subject to the same criticisms as the underlying financial statements.

 B. Changes in ratios may be highly correlated with each other.

 C. Differences in valuating elements in the numerator and denominator of ratios may cause comparisons to be misleading.

 D. When comparing the size of a ratio between periods for the same firm, conditions might have changed between the periods being compared.

CHAPTER 19

COMPOUND INTEREST EXAMPLES AND APPLICATIONS

Payment for the use of money is called interest. This chapter, which corresponds to the Appendix at the end of the text, presents the formulas that are used to evaluate streams of cash flows that are received or invested at different periods in time. The present value concept is reviewed.

CHAPTER HIGHLIGHTS

A. The amount of money borrowed or loaned is called **principal**. To **compound** interest means that the amount of interest earned during a period is added to the principal.

B. Simple interest is always calculated by using the fundamental formula, interest = principal x rate x time. Compound interest must capture the interest that is paid on not only the original principal but also the accumulated amounts of interest that are added to the principal.

C. There are two types of interest problems: one in which we need to calculate the **present value** of a future stream of cash flows; the other is the need to determine the **future value** of a stream of cash flows that begins at some point in time.

D. The future amount of an amount invested today, assuming interest is compounded, is determined by the formula:

$$F_n = P(1 + r)^n \quad \text{where}$$

F = accumulation or future value
P = the one-time investment
r = the interest rate per period
n = the number of periods from today

A shortcut approach is to use Table 1 in the text. Table 1 provides the calculations for various periods and rates of interest. To use the table, the number of periods must reflect the total compounding periods, and, correspondingly adjust the interest rate to reflect the interest per compounding period of time.

E. The present value is determined by the formula:

$$P = F_n (1 - r)^{-n}$$

Table 2 provides the calculations for the **discount factor** for various periods and rates of interest. Again, be sure the **discount rate** and the time captures all the discounting periods.

F. An **annuity** is a series of equal payments made at the beginning or end of equal periods of time. An annuity whose payments are made at the end of each period is called an **ordinary annuity**. An annuity whose payments are made at the beginning of each period is called an **annuity due**. A **deferred annuity** is one whose first payment is at some time in the future.

G. Annuities that are paid forever are called **perpetuities**.

H. An ordinary annuity, or an annuity in arrears, is a stream of periodic payments at the end of each period. The total cash will grow as a result of both the principal payments and the compounded interest payments. To determine the future value of an ordinary annuity the following formula is used:

$$F_a = [(1 + r)^{n-1} - 1]/r.$$

A shortcut is to use Table 3 at the end of the text. The table provides a factor, when multiplied by the periodic payment, yields the future value for a specified period of time.

I. To determine the present value of an annuity, Table 4 is useful. It provides factors that will equate a series of future payments to the current cash equivalent.

J. If the first payment of an annuity is at the start of the period, it is called an **annuity due**. To calculate the future value of an annuity due, one payment should be subtracted from the result using Table 3. Similarly, to calculate the present value of an annuity due, one payment should be added to the factor (n-1 time periods) found in Table 4.

K. Deferred annuities also need special attention if the tables are used. To calculate the present value of a deferred annuity, the present value of an annuity for n + d periods is determined and the value of a annuity for d periods is then subtracted.

L. The future value of a perpetuity is derived from the following formula:

$$P_a = A [1 - (1 + r)^{-n}]/ r.$$

M. The internal rate of return in a capital budget problem can be determined by the formula or by trial and error using the factors in the tables.

SELF-TEST AND PRACTICE EXERCISES

A. For each of the following six exercises, assume the interest rate is 10% compounded annually and the number of periods is three years. (Round to the nearest dollar) Record the table number and factor in the chart below:

                                            <u>Table</u>   <u>Factor</u>   <u>Answer</u>

1. The value at the end of three years of $100 invested now.

2. The present value of $133 to be received at the end of three years.

3. The value at the end of three years of a yearly payment of $100 made at the end of each year

4. The value in #3 if the annual payment is made at the beginning of each year.

5. The present value of a yearly payment of $100 made at the end of each year for three years.

6. The value in #5 if the annual payment is made at the beginning of each year.

B. For each of the following six exercises, assume the interest rate is 10%, compounded semi-annually.

                                            <u>Table</u>   <u>Factor</u>   <u>Answer</u>

1. The value at the end of three years of $100 invested now.

2. The present value of $134 to be received at the end of three years.

3. The value at the end of three years of a semiannual payment of $ 50 made at the end of each semiannual period.

4. The value in #3 if the semiannual payment is made at the beginning of each period.

5. The present value of a semiannual payment of $ 50 made at the end of each semiannual period for three years.

6. The value in #5 if the semiannual payment is made at the beginning of each semiannual period.

C. For each of the following eight questions, assume the interest rate is 5% compounded annually. Round your answers to the nearest dollar. Indicate the table you used and the factor in the chart below.

                                                        Table   Factor(s)   Answer

1. How much must be invested now to have $40,000 in ten years?

2. If $12,000 is invested now, what will be the value of the investment in 4 years?

3. How much must be invested now to provide $200,000 in two years, an additional $100,000 in two more years, and an additional $50,000 at the end of year 6?

4. How much will a firm have in its fund in five years if it deposits $30,000 now, $35,000 a year from now, $40,000 two years from now and $45,000 three years from now?

5. An investment of $6,000 will be made at the end of each year for 24 years. How much will be accumulated at the end of the 24th year?

6. A firm is going to invest $50,000 at the beginning of each year for the next ten years How much will the investment be worth at the end of the tenth year?

7. How much must be invested now to provide for an annual payment of $20,000 at the end of each year for the next seven years?

8. How much can be spent on labor saving investments that will save $6,000 now and $6,000 at the end of each year for five more years?

SOLUTIONS

A.

	Table no.	Factor	Answer
(1)	1	1.331	133
(2)	2	.751	100
(3)	3	3.31	331
(4)	3	4.64 - 1	364
(5)	4	2.487	249
(6)	4	1.735 + 1	274

B.

	Table no.	Factor	Answer
(1)	1	1.34	134
(2)	2	.7462	100
(3)	3	6.802	340
(4)	3	8.142 - 1	357
(5)	4	5.076	254
(6)	4	4.326 + 1	267

C.

	Table	Factor	Answer
(1)	2	.614	$24,560
(2)	1	1.216	$14,592
(3)	2	.907 .823 .746	$301,000
(4)	1	1.276 1.216 1.158 1.103	$176.795
(5)	3	44.502	$267,012
(6)	3	14.207 - 1	$660,350
(7)	4	5.786	$115,720
(8)	4	4.330 + 1	$31,980

STUDY PLAN

1. After mastering the study guide exercises, do the even-numbered exercises in the text. The authors do not tell you which table to use. You must determine which table to use.

2. Try to determine the internal rate of return in Exercise 30. Use trial and error and the tables.

3. Breakeven should be computed considering the time value of money. Do Exercise 40 to learn how to integrate the two concepts.

4. Review the following chart:

Problem	Table	Adjustment
1. The future value of an amount invested today	1	
2. The future value of a sum invested at the end of a period	3	
3. The future value of a sum invested at the beginning of each period	3	+1
4. The present value of a sum to be paid in some future period	2	
5. The present value of a stream of payments received at the end of each period	4	
6. The present value of a stream of payments received at the beginning of each period	4	−1